LITTLE STREAMS, BIG RIVER

China's Economic Development and
Environmental Challenges

By Chris Rynning

Table of Contents

Author's Note

The legendary ice hockey player Wayne Gretsky famously said his father told him to skate to where the puck is going, not where it has been. If applied to the world of finance, the argument would be to invest where the growth will be, rather than where it has been. It is not a perfect analogy, but captures the idea that investors have to come to China if they expect to capture future alpha returns. The puck is undeniably on its way to the Middle Kingdom, as Chinese assets are underrepresented in global asset indices. Hence diversified institutional investors do not hold the proportion of Chinese assets that the relative GDP weight predicates. The main reason for the underweighting is that the government does not freely allow international investors to directly hold Chinese equities. Chinese stock markets have been closed to international investors, and the main way to access China has been through the Hong Kong stock exchange. This is now changing.

President Xi Jinping and Premier Li Keqiang are on a path to reform the Chinese financial markets, which includes opening up the stock market for foreign investors. Continued reform will allow global funds to catch up on their China asset allocations. Financial market reform has started as both China and international investors are experimenting with quotas to invest into the Chinese stock market. In the next two to three years, the most optimistic economic observers expect significant opening up, while others think reform will take longer time. Regardless, increased demand for Chinese equities will put upward pressure on the Chinese stock market. Counterbalancing demand will be liquidity leaving China in search of global diversification and returns abroad, similarly increasing prices in whichever territory and asset class where the "Chinese puck" is going. Investors looking for alpha growth will have to be invested in China or what China demands abroad, ideally taking the elevator from the ground floor up, not getting in near the top.

While China has delivered impressive and sustained growth for over a decade, this book will argue that there is a lot more growth left in China, especially in sectors like clean technologies and energy efficiencies. I describe herein challenges for the status quo of Chinese environment, while also pointing out where opportunities abound for both policy improvement and investments alike.

Having worked on this book while stuck in Beijing traffic, I am in awe of writers everywhere. Writing is hard. I am not a writer, or a Sinologist. I am not sure this book *had to* be written, nor am I sure it has truly novel ideas, but it does hopefully bring to light some contemporary thoughts on China that can be discussed further. The more we learn about China the better, and if this book is of any contribution to "China awareness" for some, then mission accomplished.

I want to thank Christopher Pettersen, Anthony Donald and Anton Multala, who have been an immense help with my research and editing. Without their work and motivation, this book would not have been completed.

I also want to thank my children Ida and Isak for inspiring me, and my loving wife Susan for putting up with me. I love you all.

Chris Rynning, Beijing, August 2013

Preface

Flying to Beijing on a sunny Saturday in January 2013, I was enjoying the blue skies of Inner Mongolia. China had just experienced the coldest winter since "records began", which according to the Beijing government, would mean about fifty years ago. The Mongolian steppes were covered in a thin layer of white snow. The Sun, snow and blue skies gave me the warm feeling of Easter skiing, glüh-wine and oranges my young adulthood had provided me with in Norway. As the captain came on the speaker to announce "30 minutes to landing", I started to notice a brown, mountainous cloud in the distance. Flying closer, I realized we were going to enter the cloud and Beijing was not only inside of it, but potentially creating it. It dawned on me that this was no weather system, but rather a concoction of coal smoke, car emissions and urban pollution. I was looking at the gates of Beijing, the environmental Mordor of China. As we entered the capsule, the airplane started to shake and the seat belt sign came on. A stewardess apologized for the "inconvenience", and my son woke up in the seat next to me. "Are we home now?" he asked. "Not really" I said, realizing that this was no home for an asthma prone 15 year old. "We are landing soon, so get your inhaler ready and face mask on, son, we are going in".

Walking out of the plane, we were greeted by the familiar smell of burned coal, sulfur and dry dust. I noticed, however, more facemasks worn by the airport personnel than usual. Was there another bird flu epidemic I had not heard about? Approaching the masked immigration officer, I jokingly said, "Although my son has a face mask, absolutely none of us have bird flu". Quite happy with my joke, the immigration officer stared at me for what felt like an eternity, and then proceeded for two eternities to examine our passports. Eventually handing back our papers, he said: "*Son smart, you stupid, Beijing air dangerous. Goodbye!*" Thereafter we went to pick up our luggage, my son feeling quite amused and energized, and me not really knowing what to say or do. I was jet-lagged after all.

The rest of the weekend was spent indoors because the American Embassy's air quality readings were off the scale. On the 12th of January 2013, the official PM2.5 measurement reached 993 micrograms per cubic meter of tiny particulate matter, a rating roughly 4000% above World Health Organization (WHO) standards.[1] Beijing residents were consequently told to stay indoors. That day became known as the "Airpocalypse". The US Embassy pollution monitor indicated 19 days of "hazardous" pollution levels in January alone. Visibility in the city was reduced to a few hundred meters and online e-commerce sites experienced an overwhelming demand for facemasks.[2]

On the same day, over 50 flights were canceled from Beijing Capital International Airport and nine highways were closed, while state media warned how the smog could threaten economic growth.[3] In open criticism of current policies, several state media channels questioned the rationale of sacrificing the environment for the sake of economic development. As 103 high-emission companies were ordered to stop production the following week, the Beijing government also ordered government agencies and state-owned enterprises to reduce vehicle use by 30% by the end of the month. Even Beijing's Mayor declared that pollution would be the local government's top priority, and new car sales would have emission criteria to match the strictest of the European Union's emission standards.[4] With a new leadership just settling in Beijing's Zhongnanhai, this was indeed fresh ideas and new rhetoric.

This book is about China, its breathtaking development and its environment. There are China experts and economists everywhere with a plethora of interpretations and recommendations on China. Much has also been written about the Chinese environment, both by Chinese specialists and international environmental protectionists. In addition, journalists and scientists everywhere are doing a phenomenal job picking apart, criticizing and suggesting new strategies for the new Chinese leadership. This book synthesizes some of this work and aims to add a practitioner's view of China today. China is reported to spend about USD 91 billion on environmental protection annually, or 1.3% of their GDP.[5] This percentage may sound like a lot, but is too little. It is estimated that China needs to spend at least 4% of their GDP on environmentally related investments to compensate for the lack of focus on the environment in the past, while addressing current and new challenges.[6]

The story of the Chinese environment is complicated. It has a dark past and a difficult present. Although the Chinese environment has suffered, urbanization has prevailed, stimulating a rise in living standards and limiting poverty for millions. The Chinese leadership recognizes that the transformation has not been perfect and has had significant costs and flaws. It will take time before the Chinese leaders and people can together figure out and perfect their system, but we should all help China succeed. Assisting China in balancing their economic progress with global climate pressures may prove critical to our own survival. Saving the Chinese environment may also be a great investment opportunity for countries, businesses and individual investors alike.

It is imperative to understand that there is no such thing as a "One China" when discussing the country and its environment. China contains such a complex set of organizations and different levels of local and central leadership that to assume there is only one strong state leadership which creates and controls all decisions is not only wrong, but misses many of the intricate ways in which Chinese politics work. Yet, to try to understand China one must simplify its political intricacies in order to make conceptual sense, at the cost of missing out on the underlying complexity of the various interests present in this country.

I am not a scientist, an economist or an environmentalist. I am an investor. As such, my job has been to spot investment opportunities, particularly in China. Without recommending particular stocks or subsectors, this book may provide businesses and investors with some further insight as to where potential investment prospects in China may arise. International businesses that have developed products and services in Europe, the Middle East and North America, for example, will lose an opportunity of a lifetime if they do not try to enter the Chinese market. I have helped numerous western companies to come to China, and I cannot think of any business that did not benefit from it.

Opportunities in China are rife, but exist partly due to the complicated nature of the country, which is difficult to understand. In an effort to understand some of China's complexities, I will first cover the topic of urbanization, followed by a discussion on the consumers who live in cities and villages the sizes of small countries. Energy, which powers all of these developments, will then be discussed, including both non-renewable and renewable sources. The plain to see consequences of growth, pollution in all of its forms, will be illustrated. The Chinese government is well aware of the devastating effect of pollution, and with the leadership changes in Beijing, this has presented some intriguing new possibilities. Chinese media has traditionally acted as the Government's voice, but the recent pollution and political reformist shift has shown a new side of the State Council. Towards the end of this book, I will discuss a few of my own policy recommendations, paying special attention to the environmental challenges facing China and how they could be addressed. Throughout this discourse, companies and investors may find some investment ideas.

Chinese Legacy

To understand modern day China, I will for a brief moment pause at its past. In 1958, Chairman Mao Zedong launched his famous "battle against sparrows" under the "four pest plan". Speaking that year at the Communist Party Congress, he mobilized the country to wage a war against sparrows, rats, flies and mosquitos; anything that eats seeds, food or crops. With military planning, millions of Chinese were mobilized to go out and kill sparrows. The basic idea was that sparrows were reducing China's agricultural output. Nests, eggs and birds were killed in a campaign that lasted several years and decimated sparrow populations in large parts of the country.

Local scientists did point out sparrows also killed insects, but Mao shrugged it off. One man's word was enough to wage a war. The killing of sparrows contributed in this way to the famine during the Great Leap Forward, where an estimated 30-50 million people starved to death. Unscientific methods degraded the fields and the killing of sparrows contributed to massive insect infestations of both fields and grain.

Since Mao's death in 1976, many of his programs have been openly criticized by Chinese policy makers and scientists. When discussing current environmental practices in China, one must first recognize how Mao's thinking and approach left irreparable damage and lingering policy approaches in the country. To fully appreciate the Chinese philosophical view of nature, we need to go much further back than Chairman Mao. It is necessary to briefly explore the philosophical approaches to life in China, broadly practiced in Daoism, Buddhism and Confucianism.

Daoism centers on *balance in nature* and Buddhism seems to seek harmony between all *living creatures*. As this book is not about fundamental philosophical theory, I will simply leave Daoism and Buddhism for the reader to explore and judge at will, but merely conclude their core principles seem to balance rather well with the environment. While playing a central part of Chinese culture, it may also be argued that Daoism and Buddhism have been less influential on the Chinese people, and particularly Chinese politics, than Confucianism.

Confucianism as a political theory derives from the ancient philosopher, Confucius. Its fundamental principles are based upon the management and utilization of nature, people and all available resources. Scholastic consensus seems to agree Confucianism has been the most dominating philosophy in China. One can say China's urge to control and manage both human activity and nature is closely related to the legacy of Confucius, an intuitive approach for a country this vast.

Certainly, Confucius and Mao had good intentions when seeking to organize and manage the sheer scale and complexity of China. China has always had hundreds of millions of people and provinces the size of large European countries. How does one otherwise manage the diversity of nature and people? As of today, China has always been the scene of natural disasters, big and small, year after year. Chinese literature recounts floods and droughts, famine and war. The idea to control or limit natural disasters, and possibly nature itself has been an occupation of all China's rulers from ancient time up until today. The objectives and intent have also generally been good: to improve human life and living conditions for all.

While Confucian rulers have for centuries intended to mold nature for human benefit, no Chinese ruler has ever taken it upon himself to *change nature* on such a scale as Chairman Mao Zedong, using whatever means necessary. From its birth in 1949, the Chinese Communist Party took it upon itself to restructure society, humans and nature.[1] The Communist Party can celebrate more than half a century in power, and hundreds of millions of people now have access to electricity, education and enough food to eat. The most prominent economic progress and accomplishments across Chinese society can be attributed to the effective Chinese leadership during and after Deng Xiaoping's time in office. The concentrated efforts to shape both society and the natural environment during the '50s, '60s and '70s have had, and still have, disastrous consequences for China. Damming, deforestation and unsustainable farming practices have left irreparable damage on ecosystems all across the country, and people are unnecessarily suffering from it today. By condemning the Chinese environmental status today as a result of the last decade's economic leapfrog would be failing to acknowledge the strong anchoring of its Maoist past.

Mao's "war on nature" set aside both scientific research, and centuries of practical "know how" in pursuit of a Soviet-inspired utopian world. It was madness set in system. Mao actively rejected both Chinese tradition and western science when he launched his many campaigns starting in the 1950s. The objective seemed to be to master and tame nature. When alternative ideas or failures were presented to the top, persecution, coercion and pre-emptive falsifications would follow. Communes were soon competing to produce the most outrageous vegetables, fantasy yields and unheard of prosperity. Lambs were crossed with cows, wildlife was tamed and bred, wheat and corn were grown successfully together and the farmers feasted on the output. None of it was true, or sustainable.

Mao's dominative techniques and suppression of knowledge contributed to fully unsustainable practices, chaos and human suffering. Scientists, academics or practitioners with alternative views were sent to labor camps, coerced to compliance or persecuted to death. Mao upheld the view that through human struggle and coordination, nature could be harnessed and conquered.

Chinese scientists today agree these policies were directly responsible for the destruction of the environment on an unprecedented scale. It is noteworthy that Mao was of peasant origin, yet his entire approach to systems, society and nature was that of "struggle and war". He had risen to power through war and the use of military. Mao continued to manage the country in a militaristic style, opposing nature and challenging common knowledge. Mao's thoughts colored all decision-making.

With Chairman Mao, there was no room for alternative thoughts. It was a militaristic system with one ruler. It is no secret that many Chinese leaders were opposed to Mao's policies. We know this because they were all sent to labor camps or prison. Zhou Enlai, Peng Dehuai, Deng Xiaoping, and the current President Xi Jinping's father, Xi Zhongxun, were all at various points opposed to Mao's thoughts. Again, they all paid for their opposition through re-education, labor camps or political exile.

Mao established military rhetoric in the public consciousness. "Battles" were fought against floods, draughts and even mountains. Mao's own essay about *"The foolish old man who removed the mountains"* represented the human effort necessary to conquer nature, and was an example to follow. The combination of rejection of modern science, local expertise and topographic variances, in addition to the large-scale, military type attack on nature contributed to immeasurable damage to China's natural environment. China has yet to recover from the systematic over-extraction of resources the Mao era instigated.

Maoist armies cut down whole forests for wasteful steel-making schemes. They permanently damaged land values by intense farming programs, over-cropping and misguided farming practices. Ecosystems subject to massive over-cropping never recovered and permanent damage was done to wildlife habitats that will never be seen again. Overpopulation led to over-fishing, over-hunting and excessive well digging. Ground water was exhausted on an enormous scale with areas left as wastelands. The introduction of communal farming systems eliminated personal or private interest, care and responsibility for the well being of the land. Few had personal incentives to protect and preserve, and those that did, received nothing in return or were sent away.

Therefore, the current leaders must draw strength and inspiration from the former leaders, such as Deng Xiaoping and Xi Zhongxun, in order to pave the way for a sustainable future. It is of great importance for the global community that development in China continues "harmoniously" with nature, instead of raging Maoist wars to conquer it.

China today is a very different place than what Mao left behind when he died in 1976. Lessons from the Mao era are well understood in the political and scientific landscape of contemporary China. Political participation, academic freedom and the rule of law are progressing. Respect for water, land and local responsibility is taking form, however, the pressure imposed by urbanization and consumption remains daunting. Chinese citizens enjoy more freedom and local self-governance than ever before, but that in itself is not enough to repair past and recent disasters. In order to confront current environmental challenges requires boldness and sustaining economic pain.

President Xi is aware China is not perfect. He and his colleagues are working on how to improve it. The Mao era showed that social experiments can come at extraordinarily high costs. There is hope in how China's current leaders encourage intellectual and scientific freedom of expression as a means to prevent similar catastrophes in the future. Disengagement from most Maoist doctrines and many Confucian principles may prove to be difficult, yet ultimately beneficial.

Is the Climate Changing?

If one spends a week in Beijing during winter, one will no doubt acknowledge that the climate is changing, and for the worse as is made evident by the polluted air and water, sandstorms and "stinky rivers". The Chinese know their environment and climate are under extreme stress. They can see it and feel it. While they know that something must change, there is one major obstacle for all developing economies with regards to binding environmental commitments: all nations fundamentally value their national economic interests above the global environment, and China is no exception. For example, the 15th Conference of the Parties of the United Nations Convention on Climate Change in Copenhagen failed to reach any formal, let alone binding agreements, to reduce emission of greenhouse gases (GHGs). Furthermore, since the global economic slowdown in 2008, talks regarding the reduction of emissions have become increasingly difficult, as governments are preoccupied with managing unemployment and financial instability.

The Chinese government and scientific community are fully aware of the realities of global warming. Over a period of several decades, specifically from 1961 to 2007, the maximum, minimum and mean daily temperatures were gathered and analyzed to be compared with climate models. The tests were conducted by a group of Chinese scientists from the Institute of Atmospheric Physics in Beijing, and were published in the Geophysical Research Letters Journal. The results can be summarized by the statement from the lead author of the report, Zhang Xuebin, who commented that the findings were "way above what you would expect from normal fluctuations of the climate. It is quite clear and can be attributed to greenhouse gases".[2] This unflinching statement comes from the results of the temperatures that were gathered across China. For the hottest day and night of the year in 2007, the warmest annual extreme temperatures had risen by 0.92°C and 1.7°C, respectively. In parallel to this extreme heat, the coldest annual extreme temperatures had increased by 2.83°C and 4.44°C during the coldest day and night of that same year.[3]

The economic repercussions were clearly expressed by the report's co-author Qiuzi Han Wen, who said the findings would "have huge implications for China, as heat waves and droughts have already become more and more of an issue in our country". The consequences manifest themselves as increased hardships for dry-land farming due to rising scarcity of water supply. Higher demands for energy are accompanied by demand for cooling systems and a rise in "heat-induced health issues" is linked to increased temperatures, according to Qiuzi.[4] Although a severe situation, it is interesting to note that China only became the world's largest GHG emitter in 2007.[5]

While China has for some time now been the world's largest emitter of GHGs, the historical responsibility for emissions has been held by developed nations and their now affluent populations. China acknowledges that their own emissions must be reduced if the worst case scenarios of global environmental decline are to be avoided, but asks that for ethical reasons, the West must make binding commitments first. China argues that the developed economies polluted the environment as they grew wealthy, thus China should also be allowed to raise its living standards before having to cut GHGs. Simply put, Chinese leaders refuse limiting emissions before the developed countries take binding steps and act accordingly.

China's position on GHGs has been consistent for the last 20 years and largely accepted by most developmental institutions and western governments alike. However, none had foreseen China would grow this rapidly to become such a dominant GHG polluter, and that climate change would happen at such a fast pace. While China's GHG intensity, emissions per unit of economic output, is improving and the average per capita emission remains below the US, its emissions are high compared to other countries and certainly the highest in absolute terms.[6] Then again, the United States remains by far the largest historical carbon polluter to date.

While studying the Chinese government's own GHG objectives, it is very clear that emissions are taken seriously. Yet, emissions will not take priority over China's economic and other national interests. Only where climate change does not impair China's economic development can we expect to see material willingness to introduce legislation, or any type of binding agreements in the nearby future. China's policies are generally aimed at national development, including poverty eradication. GHG discussions are a side topic when you are trying to provide food, energy and basic infrastructure to several hundred million people. For this reason alone, the Chinese government is extraordinarily sensitive to any form of external political interference.

The Chinese policies on renewable energy, such as solar and wind, must be seen as more of an effort to become increasingly energy independent, rather than as shorter-term policies on combating GHG emissions. Technological leadership, market development and economic returns are also objectives mentioned in Government speeches on sustainable development. China is certainly seeing a market opportunity in developing cleaner technologies, thus policies for a greener, more sustainable development are only partly driven by a desire to reduce emissions. As long as China's per capita emissions remain relatively low, and the climate does not undergo a cataclysmic change, then the Chinese people and government will argue China's global responsibility towards remedying climate change is quite small. At the same time, China is not strictly-speaking a developing country, with millions of wealthy individuals and rapidly emerging middle-class consumers. For this segment of the population, the argument that China has a low per capita GHG pollution profile is less convincing. For this group of people and the cities they typically inhabit, such as Beijing, Shanghai and Shenzhen, other stricter regulations and commitments could, and should, apply now.

Recently an outlet for people concerned with the environment emerged in the form of social media. Regular Chinese media outlets are one of the most controlled sectors in China. For years, I never read Chinese media, expecting to find nothing but propaganda. However, since the beginning of 2013, I have noticed that Chinese media is increasingly critical and outspoken, especially on the environmental status and are in fact more openly critical about social, environmental and even political issues. Every day one can read state newspapers and online articles harshly critical of industries, citizens and government officials that do not follow regulations and policies.

The notable shift in local media's coverage has been amplified by the poor Beijing air quality and the infamous pigs found floating in a Shanghai river in the spring of 2013. It is not a coincidence that this development is happening in parallel with top political leadership changes. President Xi Jinping and Premier Li Keqiang have clearly set out on a campaign to root out corruption and non-performance, through reform and restructuring. As much as they are using the media to instigate changes, media has also taken a stronger and more critical view on many aspects of Chinese society.

Chinese citizens know a lot about their environment. They can see and feel the degradation, and it does not take the media or a scientist to tell them that the state of affairs is not sustainable. What is new, however, is they can now also read about it in the state media, and those with Internet access can read critical articles concerning China in both domestic and foreign media in Mandarin and English. The assumption that Chinese citizens do not know what is going on in their country, or in certain sub-sectors such as environmental deterioration, is false. If you speak to the Chinese, most of them will hold quite an open and cynical view on the domestic environment, and industrial pollution in particular. Social media with its instant, free and vast reach is changing the way the Government acts and how citizens air their discontent. It is allowed to criticize; in fact it is encouraged to criticize certain aspects, as long as the Communist Party's legitimacy is not challenged.

In other words, you may complain about an official, but you cannot complain about the Party or system. The Party is still untouchable, but companies and politicians are not. People on the street generally do not want an end to the Communist Party. They primarily want improved financial and environmental living conditions, and there is broad support that the Communist Party provides just that. The minute new jobs are insufficient or growth falls dramatically, that support may dwindle. Hence, the Chinese leadership's top priority is growth that sustains employment rates, shifting from polluting industries to value added services.

Chinese people whom are employed also consume. Chinese consumers, by sheer number and purchasing power, hold a key to global technological development and investments in research and development. Chinese consumers are in a unique place to influence products and services globally. Whatever Chinese consumers *want*, it will be developed. If 1.3 billion consumers, or even a small segment of them want products and services to facilitate a better environment, then that will help determine what is developed and shipped around the world. No other country is in a similar position of scale and absolute demand, capable of influencing global production and shipment patterns. India may have been in such a position a few years back, but it has not taken off in the same way China has. India's caste system, lacking infrastructure and long political processes have so far hindered economic and middle class progress on an equal scale with China, but if properly addressed, India may soon play a comparable role. In the meantime, the world looks to China.

The world of investment and finance has been transfixed in the last 10 years on the economic rise of China. Where are the asset bubbles? When will they burst? In every quarter for the last 10 years, there has been a senior economist at a bank in Europe or the US predicting a "hard landing" in China. For every prediction of an economic recession in China or a bubble bursting, China has under-promised and over-delivered. Chinese politicians are experts in lowering the goals to the point where they are quite certain that they can deliver, even if

China has to launch excessive stimulus packages for job creation and meeting stated gross domestic product (GDP) growth figures.

Even during the years of the global financial crises in 2008 and 2009, China delivered economic growth above 7%, providing China's approximate 10 million annual university graduates with new jobs. A continued key element of Chinese GDP growth, and therefore world economic growth, is Chinese state fixed asset investments (FAI). Simply by relying on China's commitment to green infrastructure, another decade of GDP growth rates around 7% or above is more than likely. The head of China's National Bureau of Statistics, the state ministerial statistics agency, Ma Jiantang, has recommended China to aim for a 7-8% annual growth figure for the next decade. Other prominent economists, like David Daokui Li of Tsinghua University, think that China will revert to a higher GDP growth curve of about 8-9% in the latter half of this decade, driven by the growth of both basic infrastructure investments and the service economy.

China's growth will be driven by a myriad of investments in basic infrastructure. Simply by continuing to invest in water irrigation, sewage treatment, railway, electric charging stations and mass transportation, China can deliver on its GDP growth targets. The only doubt can then be twofold: do they *want* to build this infrastructure and can they *pay* for it? There is no doubt in my mind China has both the political will and financial capability to do so. Where there is will and capability, there typically are results.

Growth in China is not going to be a straight line of economic home runs every year. China and the world will have to accept setbacks or significant asset price corrections, either set off by political crises, military conflicts, accidents or "black swans". When this happens, some economists' prediction of "bust and hard landing" will be "right", and they will be the gurus of their time. They will be correct; in the same fashion a broken analog clock shows the right time twice a day. It will happen. However, in the joy of being correct, one might miss the opportunity of a lifetime to invest into what is one of the largest economic transformations in history.

The first business I helped bring to China was Elkem ASA, a large diversified metal and materials conglomerate from Norway. The business case was clear: Elkem imported raw materials from China to Norway and the US, in order to manufacture products there, for export back to Asia. It did not make economic sense to import raw materials from Asia to Europe and then export it all back to Asia. If anything, it was costly and bad for the environment. After a long and frustrating process, the board of Elkem approved acquiring land and buildings in a remote location of the Ningxia Autonomous region of China, near the raw materials themselves. The relocation of manufacturing from Norway to Ningxia immediately cut input and delivery costs, while prices to customers were kept on par. In other words, margins ballooned. While on a small scale, the investment was phenomenally successful and the payback time was less than five years, a great result within the sector of industrial processing. In 2010, Elkem was bought by China National Bluestar, a Chinese-state owned enterprise. With a sale to the Chinese state, Elkem was in many ways coming full circle from its entry to China in the 1990s. The shareholders of Elkem ultimately got handsomely paid by the Chinese state for their shares, which is not bad for a company that somewhat reluctantly entered China in 1996. By being visible in China and improving profitability, Elkem created new and unexpected exit opportunities for their shareholders.

Later I invested in a company called Halosource, a Seattle, Washington based manufacturer of different water purification technologies and products, including so-called "point of use" water treatment cartridges. Post investing in the company I assisted them in expanding their manufacturing capacity in Shanghai, significantly lowering their cost of production. Halosource was awarded licenses from the Chinese Ministry of Health, allowing them to start selling their products in China. In 2010, much fueled by their market position in China, Halosource was able to list on the London Stock Exchange, thus raising further financing through accessing new institutional investors. Their China strategy opened new financing venues for the company as well as opening new markets.

A similar example is Aqualyng, a Norwegian based desalination company, which converts seawater to fresh water through reverse osmosis technology. The company had traditionally tried to sell its technology to international customers. A technology and solution sales strategy is quite lumpy, from a cash flow perspective, so the company changed its business model from selling technology installations to essentially becoming a water producer in cooperation with local partners. The first, and to date, only market it has penetrated on a larger scale is China. The company entered into a so-called joint venture with the Chinese government where they together built one of the largest water desalination plants in the world, using Aqualyng technology, not far from Tianjin city in northern China. Aqualyng's China strategy has been the single most important factor in attracting further financing and talent to the business. The reason for mentioning these cases above is that the companies that tend to understand and embrace China are likely to attract international investor attention, in addition to addressing real local demand.

The water companies are addressing real problems in China. Consider that China is estimated to only have about 1,730 cubic meters of fresh water per person. The UN deems countries being close to the 1,700 cubic meter-level to be "stressed".[7] The situation is worse in northern China, where half of China's people, most of its coal and only 20% of its water are located. Shanxi Province, the nation's biggest coal base, with about 28% of China's coal production, has per capita water resources of merely 347 cubic meters, less than the Middle Eastern nation of Oman. Inner Mongolia and Shaanxi, which together contribute 40% of coal output, have less than 1,700 cubic meters per person.[8] Surely, this is both incredibly frightening as well as signaling massive opportunities to help and invest?

Chinese rivers are either drying up, being contaminated or under severe stress. China needs water to mine coal, and without coal both the economy and the energy sectors come to a stop. The coal industry employs approximately 17% of China's water supply, mainly in the northern, dry provinces.[9] As we will discuss later, the Chinese government needs to significantly expand coal-fired energy production. Without water this will not happen and current solutions are not sustainable by any means. Without adequate water resources, China will not be able to meet its long-term GDP growth targets.

There is no doubt in scientists' view that the Earth's climate is changing, and that is the only perspective we should seriously consider. What media, investors or celebrities say on this particular issue is less important. I recommend we trust the scientists on this one. However, the purpose of this book is not to debate over the effects or validity of global warming, but rather the real and local environmental issues in China; what China's deteriorating environment means for all of us and how it can be dealt with, even taken advantage of. No one knows what the consequences may be from the current human activities on Earth. We know the earth has been through a lot in the past with meteoric storms and ice ages. What happens next no one knows. Maybe that is why the Chinese are busy mastering how to land on the moon and populating Mars? I have not booked my ticket to Mars yet, but if I do, it might very well be on a Chinese travel site.

Who is to Blame for the Poor Environment?

With increased awareness about pollution and the related facts, public outrage and demands for accountability have erupted across China. Ma Jun, founder of the Institute of Public and Environmental Affairs in Beijing, was quoted in state media saying, "The PM2.5 issue has aroused extensive public concern. Before concern was raised in certain specific cases, now it is about the air people breathe and the water they drink, which affect hundreds of millions of people".[10] People are beginning to notice that their public demands are somewhat addressed. By January 2013, more than 70 cities in China were releasing their PM2.5 data in real time over digital media.[11] There is no escape from it even if you stay at home, the pollution is everywhere. However, with a country as expansive and complicated as China, who is to blame for the environment?

Individuals have often been praised as the solution to pollution. In China, the situation is not much different from the west. A big debate issue is the philosophical question of individual versus corporate responsibility for a polluted environment. The rhetoric in Chinese state media seems to be that we are all to blame for the poor air quality and that we all need to make an effort in cleaning up the environment. There is a certain line of logic to be followed in the Chinese state press, such as the state-owned *China Daily* newspaper calling for a "joint effort" to fight air pollution, noting "[tackling] air pollution requires input from individuals as well as officials".[12] The paper urges citizens to use public transportation and drive less, thus indicating that an individual's greatest contribution to lessening air pollution is derived from their mode of transport. It seems intuitive to urge citizens to use public transportation and drive less, and for the Government to facilitate such transportation needs. In 2013, President Xi reformed decision-making for inter-city train construction approvals to be made at a local level, thus approval is no longer required on the state-level.[13] As Beijing pushes for reform and decentralization, Du Shaozhong, the Deputy Director of the Beijing Municipal Environmental Protection Administration emphasized the duty of the individuals in March 2013 by saying that "[everyone] is responsible for creating air pollution. No one will act if we all just place our hopes in others".[14] Intuition and common sense, yes, but is this the right approach?

While there is truth to the argument that we can all do something, fundamentally the individual contribution to local and global pollution is tiny when compared to the industrial and structurally based pollution in China. It is private companies and state-owned enterprises that represent the vast majority of pollution. Moreover, Beijing City's own contribution also seems relatively small as it has either shut down or relocated its most polluting industries to other regions. In Beijing, the air pollution was previously attributed to heavy-duty vehicles such as trucks and buses, where 61% of particulate matter originated from heavy-duty vehicles compared to only 22% for passenger vehicles. Zhou Rong, a climate and energy project manager for Greenpeace China argues, "The major problem is still in the structure of the economy and energy consumption, which cannot be changed by ordinary people".[15] All people can agree that they can participate and do something on a personal level; however, over half of the respondents in a 2011 World Wide Fund for Nature survey agreed that broader environmental protection is "at least somewhat" of a government responsibility.[16]

Pollution is also an economic and ethical responsibility held by Chinese businesses, local and foreign. All business activities in China are accountable for polluting, however, few as significantly as the coal burning electricity plants. The World Bank estimates that coal burning accounts for 19% of all air pollution, compared to only 6% from all vehicles according to a Greenpeace and Peking University study.[17] When investing in clean technologies, companies with strong government support tend to be more successful. If they also are tailored for local demand or problems, the probability for success is greater. This sounds obvious, and in many ways it is. There is a subtle observation here though, where China is somewhat different from American and European markets.

In the West, a lot of clean technology is driven by global issues such as greenhouse gas emissions, the corresponding climate change and generally the satisfaction of doing the right thing. These issues may sometimes seem somewhat distant for the average consumer. In China, policies, consumption and even investing is more driven by tangible matters like much needed cost reduction or "fix it" solutions to observable problems. It might be cleaning a "stinky" and dead river, or related to solving a local energy supply shortage causing electricity "black outs". An apparent problem is easy for a mayor or a governor to politically support, especially if the politicians have been made personally responsible for improvement in their county or province. Solutions here are often tailored to a city or a province; not necessarily mass-produced, yet economies of scale often apply nonetheless due to China's sheer size. China clean tech investing is driven mainly by applying a solution to an observable problem, not a loft policy or feel good factor.

In the beginning of 2013, as the Chinese National Congress was about to start in Beijing, the combination of sand storms and smog drew away attention from the appointment of the new President Xi Jinping and Prime Minister Li Keqiang, and onto the issue of severe environmental stress. Social media overflowed with criticism and jokes about PM2.5 levels, which were literally off the scale as the American Embassy reported pollution levels "Beyond Index".[18] Beijing experienced an average of 196 micrograms per cubic meter of particulate matter in January of 2013.[19] The aforementioned Beijing "Airpocalypse" also peaked at a PM2.5 concentration of 993.

To clarify, the PM2.5 air quality measure refers to the size and concentration of particles in the air. The specific reference to "2.5" indicates that the particle must be smaller than 2.5 micrometers, essentially one-thirtieth the size of a human hair. The concentration refers to the number of particles recorded per cubic meter of air. The particles are a combination of solid particles to liquid droplets from automobiles, buses, trucks and general industry. Binary chemical compounds, such as sulfur dioxide or nitrogen oxide, can also combine as PM2.5 particles through chemical reactions. These particles are typically emitted from the combustion process when burning coal or oil in various combustion engines that you find in vehicles, ships or airplanes. All these particles can penetrate deep into lungs and create serious health risks.[20]

As a measure of comparison, a smoking lounge in an American airport has top readings of approximately 166 micrograms per cubic meter.[21] No one could imagine living in an airport smoking lounge, but that is the reality for Beijing residents during prolonged periods of smog. In addition, the

WHO has set its 24-hour mean guideline for PM2.5 exposure at a concentration of 25 micrograms per cubic meter.[22] Similarly, the EU recommends that the levels should not exceed an annual average of 25 micrograms per cubic meter.[23]

By any standards, the Beijing levels are unsustainably high, in part because the city finds itself in an unfortunate location. Beijing is surrounded by the provinces of Hebei and Shandong, which consume more coal than the entire United States of America annually.[24] In preparation for the 2008 Beijing Olympics, a large number of factories were moved out of the city to Hebei province, including Shougang steel plant, once the largest industrial polluter in Beijing. A new USD 10.8 billion plant was built only a few kilometers outside of Beijing. When southern winds come through Hebei and Shandong, the percentage of airborne pollutants in the capital can soar by 50-70%.[25] The pollutants are consequently trapped against the mountain range surrounding Beijing.[26] The January 2013 smog did not only affect Beijing, but covered an estimated area of 1.3 million square kilometers across 10 municipalities and provinces, stretching down to the central Sichuan province.[27]

I live just outside the Beijing city center, where it seems that the air quality is worse than in the city center itself, particularly during winter. Inside the city, there are no coal-fired plants and little industrial or residential pollution. In the Beijing suburbs, up to 70% of local housing have coal-fired stoves and you will find thousands of small-scale industrial operations with their own coal-fired boilers to generate cheap electricity. The pollution from these boilers and stoves is especially intense during the winter and create a harmful local environment. Shanghai and Hong Kong face similar challenges, although Chinese citizens joke about Beijing's air being "hazardous," while Shanghai pollution levels are only rated "unhealthy".[28] Hong Kong air quality monitoring stations at "Mong Kok" and "Central" have also recorded "severe" pollution levels in 2013, as air was coming down from the mainland and "got stuck" between the city's mountain peaks and skyscrapers.[29]The cost of pollution is difficult to estimate, as it reaches beyond deaths and illness to delays and inefficiencies. The World Bank estimates that China's GDP is reduced by 5-6% on an annual basis due to a combination of premature deaths, severe healthcare costs and material damages.[30] Another study highlighted that outdoor air pollution costs an estimated RMB 500 billion annually in healthcare costs, with more than 300,000 premature deaths and 20 million patients with respiratory diseases accounted for.[31]

In open criticism of current policies, several state media channels began questioning the rationale of sacrificing the environment for the sake of economic development. As 103 high-emissions companies were told to stop production, the Beijing government ordered its administrative agencies and state owned enterprises to reduce vehicle use by 30%.[32] Beijing's mayor declared that "[pollution] would be the local government's top priority" and that new car sales would have emission criteria to match European Union standards. State planners and researchers stated publically that it is the governments' responsibility to lead the way for improving air quality. Jiang Kejun, a researcher at the NDRC's Energy Research Institute, noted that fuel prices must be increased, and while it is the consumers who will bear the burden of more expensive fuel, it is the Government that must first set the standards from which companies and consumers can follow.[33] As a result, responsibility for the Beijing smog is squarely placed in the Government's lap.

The Beijing government reacted quickly and with a number of measures in early 2013. The so-called "Clean Air Action Plan" was quickly launched in order to specifically reduce Beijing's air pollutant tally by 2%. The goals are expected to be achieved by the end of 2013, with specific undertakings such as replacing coal-fired boilers and removing 180,000 old vehicles from Beijing's roads.[34] Although the government has already begun to set new and improved measures, a public debate still continues on how it intends to finance many of these projects. The "Beautiful China" environmental campaign adopted by the National People's Congress under former President Hu Jintao was aimed at creating economic growth without sacrificing the environment, while the 'Harmonious Society' campaign was steered more towards raising minimum income.[35] President Xi Jinping has said that while one has to value the past, we now need to embrace a new "China Dream", combining economic growth for everyone and simultaneously cleaning up China's air, water and soil.[36] The pollution scandals of early 2013 have forced both local and central governments to recognize environmental issues and to provide accurate data to the public, rather than trying to withhold data. A shift away from exclusive focus on economic growth to also combatting sources of pollution is quite remarkable in a Chinese context. It also highlights the responsibility of the Government in its duty to deal with air and all other forms of pollution.

While appealing to Chinese citizens, for the Government to make a real difference to air quality in China, the State Council must impose strict measures to reduce coal-related emissions and controls of the smaller, emission heavy industries. This will be challenging, since coal consumption is scheduled to rise significantly over the next decade. If China were able to reduce coal consumption to 5% annual growth, from its current 8% goal, then total consumption would still peak at 6 billion tons annually, up from the current level of 3.8 billion tons. Some experts in China fear coal consumption could reach 10 billion tons.[37]

Similarly, vehicle figures could easily quadruple by 2030, reaching 400 million vehicles. As a consequence, China must hurry and build railways and subways in order to compensate for this potential surge in vehicle emissions. The current target, which must be raised further, is to build 140,000 kilometers of rail and 7,000 km of subway by 2020, up from 90,000 km and 2,000 km respectively today. This expansion would only bring China to 12.5% of the railway and subway average of developed countries, and to only 20% of developed country standards on a per capita basis.[38] These objectives are what drive bullish Chinese GDP estimates, while the "China Bears" doubt the resolve, ability and payment capacity for China to deliver.

Pluralistic China

Although embryonic, the Chinese public's awareness of the environment extends back several years. In February 2008, a dozen of environmental activists raided the cafeteria of Microsoft's Beijing headquarters. The activists had assembled to protest and raise attention over the use of 63 billion disposable chopsticks each year.[39] Chopsticks are typically made of wood and are commonly available in restaurants in China. However, their frequent use and disposal stresses forest populations. One of the activists, a 26-year-old named Cao Yu, dressed-up as an orangutan and proclaimed "Disposable chopsticks are destroying China's forests. We must protest this pointless waste!" This Greenpeace-organized event got a lot of media coverage and is one of many increasingly visual efforts used to raise public attention for environmental issues in China.

Environmental awareness seems to spike with celebrity support, such as with the popular winner of "Super Girl", the Chinese version of "American Idol". A recent winner, Li Yuchun, was quoted saying "I use energy-saving lights at home, and I resolutely protest the use of disposable chopsticks". Further celebrity endorsement include Xiao Wei, the lead singer of the Chinese rock group "Catcher in the Rye", who is assisting Greenpeace China in a "Bring Your Own Chopstick" campaign.[40] The aim is to urge fans of the band, and the public to bring their own chopsticks to restaurants in hopes of discouraging the use of disposable chopsticks.

Such efforts to raise awareness appear to provide encouraging results. China's Ministry of Commerce has repeatedly urged restaurants to reduce the use of disposable chopsticks. After the campaigns of 2008, several hundred Beijing restaurants have said they will quit using disposable chopsticks. Large companies, such as Microsoft, Intel and IBM have also pledged support to the campaigns. Moreover, in December 2008, the Ministry of Commerce issued guidelines for restaurants to "reduce the use of disposable chopsticks".[41] Concrete measures are thus being taken in order to reduce the pressure on the environment. In this sense, activist and celebrity pressure has had a significant effect.

While China is not only playing catch up economically, it is also improving in terms of public debate and allowing the media to be a watchdog in the interest of the general public. There are signs suggesting that China is making significant progress. With the change of Chinese political leadership in 2013, state-run newspapers have begun to write articles more critical of the Government. When the Chinese Environmental Ministry refused to publish soil pollution data in the beginning of the year, on grounds of soil data being "state secrets", some state newspapers and their editors were outraged. Below are some examples of what state newspapers wrote:

> The *People's Daily's* editor wrote: "State Secrets is the magic phrase for rejecting disclosure of information. Is it because it involves secrets that it can't be revealed, or is it simply because you're afraid of triggering dissatisfaction? Covering this up only makes people think: We're being lied to."

> The *China Youth Daily* stated the decision was "unreasonable" and releasing information on polluted soil will not influence national defense construction and endanger national security".

The *Guangzhou Daily* wrote: "If one thinks that releasing sensitive data will trigger public panic and affect social stability, one is looking down upon the public literacy."

Finally, the editor-in-chief of the *Global Times* magazine wrote: "China has too many secrets, and secrets become bombs in the end. The government should be unswerving in its pursuit of greater transparency".[42]

You can make what you want of these statements, but one cannot say they do not deal with some very real issues in China, such as transparency and the Government's lack of public interest. Cynics may argue allowing the media reaction is simply lip service, or fits with the Chinese saying of "deal with one to show one hundred" - meaning you deal with the little things so that the big things are left alone. In light of recent crack downs on the shadow banking system and the health care industry such as the legal pursuit of the pharmaceutical company GlaxoSmithKline, the perception of state criticism seems to be set aside. Clearly there is a change in both the way state media are allowed to criticize and the resolve of the new leadership to implement change.[43] In my experience, most foreign based observers are relatively uninformed about how much public debate and discontent is actually allowed in China, particularly on the Internet but increasingly so in traditional forms of media such as newspapers, TV and radio.

Regularly, protests regarding environmental accidents and crimes are broadly reported, at least locally. For example, in

2012, Jiangsu province, 14 people pleaded guilty to instigating a riot after raising concerns that a Japanese company called "Oji Paper" did not properly treat wastewater before discharging it into the sea. State media reported that 90 police officers were injured during the ensuing riots, along with significant property loss.[44] The Government apparently allowed the protests to go ahead, partly to allow people to blow off steam, and some might even argue it was partly due to the company's nationality. When speaking to Chinese people about human rights, they are more often inclined to talk about the human right to have clean air, sanitary water and safe food, while not being concerned with voting rights. Most think a strong, central Communist Party is best equipped to provide them these bare necessities in such a huge and diverse country. Assuming systemic corruption can be better handled, there are compelling reasons to think so.

During the spring of 2013, state media was reporting daily on Chinese pollution and its consequences. Reporters and commentators were calling for more Government transparency and corrective action to combat pollution. State newspapers continued throughout this period to run critical articles on the need to address the source of pollution, not only treat local consequences. The state-owned *People's Daily* newspaper reported on the status of the most polluted of the large cities in China. The *Global Times* newspaper reported on public calls to shift development away from growth towards sustainability. The *People's Youth Daily* wrote the harsh headline "More suffocating than the haze is the weakness in government response".[45] Public health officials chimed in and spoke both in newspapers and on television about the hidden economic costs of respiratory diseases and cancer.[46] Conversely, I could not see that the western media had reported meaningfully on this change in Chinese attitude and reporting practices.

Floating pigs in a river, yes. Analysis of state criticism, generally no. Nevertheless, in March 2013, the state run *People's Daily* newspaper ran a front-page editorial with the headline "A Beautiful China Starts with Healthy Breathing" a pun on the former president's vision for China. *People's Daily* continued with "The vast, unmoving haze has obscured our vision, but it has made the urgency of pollution control clearer to us". Post-crisis measures "cannot replace systematic, scientific, efficient and powerful management of the problem at its source".[47] The same week a state media commentator said that *"Everyone is the victim of polluted air, and everyone is capable of reducing the smoggy air. Environment protection policies should be strengthened. Governmental departments should take the lead and drive official cars less frequently".* [48]

While more state criticism appears in newspapers, it is nothing compared to what appears in social media and discussions over lunch and dinner tables here. From my 15 years in China, it is easy to see that the new leaders allow more criticism of the state and the Government, particularly with regards to the environment. China's leaders seem to think that they can wait with some reforms, but they cannot wait to deal with clean air, water and safe food. The time for that is now, even if it includes blowing off steam towards the government.

Consider the following statements in early 2013 from the *Global Times* paper, who consistently referred to the cryptic term "crazy fog":

"In the past, the government handled pollution-related information in a 'low-key' manner. It made the choice between environmental protection and development on behalf of the people. The public doesn't buy this line of reasoning and it has led to conflicts." The public is apparently willing to reconsider the nation's economic growth "fixation". *Global Times* stated "[the] people should grasp both the importance of economic growth and the urgency of basic environmental protection. This difficult choice should be decided in a genuinely democratic manner".[49]

Pretty strong and encouraging language from a leading communist party spokesperson in one of the leading news channels, would you not agree? Beyond editors and environmental specialists voicing their concern and unhappiness with Beijing air quality, the media has also continuously reported on popular anger over air quality. It is one thing to report on air quality, but it is another thing entirely to report on public discontent. It goes beyond this book to provide a full picture of what was complained about, but most local observers will agree that state media comments frequently on very unhappy Chinese micro-bloggers and their online communities. It is unfortunate that there seems to a perception in the West that Chinese do not know about scandals or inefficiencies in their country, and that they are not allowed to voice their discontent or protest about it. This view is simply uninformed at best. There are daily protests and grass root movements in China on a variety of issues. Last year I noticed several street protests surrounding waste plants in Dalian and Xiamen, and the episodes surrounding the Shanghai high-speed rail accidents in 2012 gave rise to wide spread public criticism and protests.[50] These protests tend to influence and change policy.

This said, the key reason why environmental protests are

allowed alongside land and labor disputes is how they tend to be apolitical in nature. There might be serious criticism about the Government and certain officials, but there are no calls for a different political system or the removal of the Chinese Communist Party. The protests and criticism that exist in the media are careful not to call into question the system itself. Although requests for increased efforts, transparency and accountability are accepted, it is not permitted to ask for systemic change. These two things are different, and there is a clear line between them.

No one in China is asking publically for political or system change without consequences, but there is wide acceptance in the Chinese public for the current political system, and patience with the fact that the system breaks down from time to time. Protests typically either call for economic compensation or for certain leaders or developers to resign. Protests are frequently event-driven and call for inflicted unfairness to be corrected. Most, if not all, protests and criticism that occurred in the beginning of 2013 demanded environmental rights and particular consequences, not systemic change. Environmental complaints are not new: the Ministry of Environment reported over 300,000 environmental complaints during the previous 11th Five-Year Plan, with 2,614 administrative decisions re-examined, 980 administrative court cases concerning environmental damage and 30 criminal cases.[51]

The state-owned *China Daily* newspaper published a life quality report in 2012, which merits some attention. The key question was to assess life happiness and how it had varied over the last few years. Only 1% of those surveyed stated their quality of life had greatly improved, 20% stated their quality of life had improved slightly, while over 33% stated they felt no change in their lives now compared to a few years ago. I was surprised to read that *over 40%* stated that their lives were worse now.[52] These respondents quoted the main reasons being high medical expenses, rising housing prices, aging insecurity and general price pressures. This was a state reported survey where no facts were hidden, and may explain why Beijing itself is calling for reform.

The World Wildlife Foundation published a report in 2011 on environmental behavior and attitudes of Chinese consumers. The respondents were mainly urban residents aged between 15 and 55 years old. The survey concluded that environmental protection was still not a real factor when Chinese consumers make purchasing decisions. This suggests that environmental protection is perceived as a government, not a private concern. Yet more than 80% of respondents reported that they were focusing on electricity and water conservation in their homes, and most respondents also stated that they pay "some" or "great" attention to environmental campaigns. They also said campaigns or activities were most effective when recommended by a friend as opposed to ones solicited via the media.[53] In layman's terms, Chinese consumers seemed more driven by cost considerations in energy conservation, more than simply "doing the right thing." The smog in early 2013 changed attitudes in Beijing, as it became legitimate to speak of pollution, its costs and openly discuss what can be done to improve the environment.

On the surface, Chinese officials, and very often the public itself, will repeat Government phrases, such as "This policy is good for economic development". Probed deeper, they will either disclose that they may not in fact know much about the details of the topic itself, or reveal knowledge and opinions about the policy which are at odds with certain aspects of the actual policy. It is in these underlying opinions and objectives that China is not only understood, but actually governed. For example, "The Nature Conservancy" (TNC) is a Chinese non-governmental organization (NGO), which has a reputation of being close to the Government. In fact, it has been openly criticized for its close cooperation with the state. This position is somewhat counter-intuitive given its Chinese name is literally the "American Nature Conservancy Association". The very fact that it is an American-sponsored NGO makes it quite difficult for them to cooperate with the Chinese state. However, rather than to be in opposition to the Government, TNC has decided to become part of the governmental policy process. Their aim is to influence and help the Government make the right decisions. TNC and the state seem to regard each other as partners in a similar way which UNESCO and the World Heritage Sites look at themselves as part government-owned, part government-caretakers. In recent years, Chinese NGOs also seem increasingly aligned with state media in bringing forth stories that expose corruption or pollution of the environment. For media it sells ad space, and for the NGOs it means power to change or influence decisions. It is a strange but not uncommon form of political symbiosis.

Parts of western media would be better off by rethinking its categorical criticism of China as an authoritarian, non-democratic state, because it simply does not exist. Chinese decision-making is indeed quite pluralistic and continues to become more liberal and reform-conscious every day. There is a phenomenal amount of local and regional consensus-based decision- and policy-making, where both local and state leaders are able to exchange views and opinions. This relationship has already manifested itself in a democratic style of decision-making on most levels of the Communist Party, and is amplified among local governments and town villages. Again, what the different players seem to have in common, however, is that they do not aim to threaten the legitimacy of the Chinese Communist Party. Quite the opposite, the stakeholders see themselves either as partners of the state or as active members of the Communist Party. While western politicians and the media are predisposed to discuss the flaws of China, many are missing the fast-paced change of political discourse, which is happening right in front of their eyes. Rather than looking for western democratic structures, one should instead understand and report on the vast political multiplicity one can see the contours of in China already.

Policy in China is the result of several different ministries bargaining, influenced by leaders' personalities and agendas, and consequently implemented in multiple ways by provincial and local governments. Thereafter, every policy may either be undermined by neglect or opposed by an effort to change it through incorporating new and local considerations. Delegated Government authorities and NGOs that fight for its survival can be powerful players and agents for change. Fragmented or bureaucratized systems also allow for alliances to form, providing political power to seemingly powerless individuals or groups. Within this framework, passion, shared beliefs and hard work are also agents of change and influence.

Stakeholders in China do not generally challenge the ultimate power of the Communist Party, or the broader goals of "Economic Growth"; "Harmony and Prosperity" and "Develop the West".[54] That does not mean to say there is no opposition in China. While a confrontation against the broader objectives would be doomed from the start, it does not mean that there is no political debate happening in China. Opposition in China has centered on components of the grander plans, their implementation and corruption within. The fact remains that a huge variety of stakeholders exists, and that barriers to enter "the opposition" continuously are lowered. The Chinese political system is certainly evolving towards more participation, if not democratization as the West knows it.

It is a paradox that China has some of the strictest environmental laws in the Far East, if not all of Asia. It is in the enforcement and implementation of these laws where China falls short. Current environmental laws date back to the early 1980s when basic institutions were established to protect and monitor the environment. As described by Sinkule and Ortolano in their now iconic 1995 paper on environmental policies in China, the original law described the three "magic weapons" of "environmental impact assessments", "liability for discharges" and a holistic "design, build and operate" paradigm.[55] The laws have been managed by various departments and ministries throughout the 80s and 90s, although all the ministerial variations were seen to be of weak standing and low general priority.

One would have thought that the introduction of criminalization through modifications of the laws in the late 1990s would have had a material impact on people and companies' behavior, but that would be an overstatement. China has, however, continued to issue new standards and regulations, and combined an up-to-date and credible legal framework for environmental protection. The laws cover most areas of concern from emissions to fisheries, wildlife, forestry and waste.

Possibly the most potent law passed in the last 10 years has been the Environmental Impact Assessment Law, which included a provision that allowed people and organizations to review and criticize projects publicly. While the law has been largely ineffective in stopping unwanted projects, it has created an avenue for people and organizations to legitimately be involved.[56] Environmentalists are using this law as one of several ways to acquire insight into projects and also to create debate over development. However, overall one must conclude the implementation and enforcement of the environmental laws in China traditionally has been weak. Developers and politicians alike seem to find loopholes and ways around the law. Widespread corruption and conflicting objectives lead to polluting mines being shut down, only to re-open again shortly after. Developments and infrastructure are built with little to no environmental impact assessment if they meet other development or economic objectives instead.

In 2011, the Intermediate People's Court accepted a landmark lawsuit. A number of non-governmental organizations were demanding compensation from two companies that had allegedly been dumping chemicals. Two organizations called "Friends of Nature" and "Chongqing Green Volunteer Association" filed charges against Luliang Chemical Industry Company and Luliang Peace Technology Company.[57] The only public interest litigation case we know before this particular case involved the "All-China Environment Federation", an organization under the Ministry of Environmental Protection, which targeted companies that were allegedly dumping chromium, contaminated water near the Chachong Water Reservoir, consequently leaking into the Nanpan River. The contaminated water leaked into the water supply causing human and animal deaths, cancer and illness. Seven individuals received jail terms as a result. From these landmark cases, a more litigious process is forming.

The Standing Committee of the National People's Congress has opened up for legally registered organizations to file complaints and law suits freely, including environmental cases. Environmental groups in China were allowed to form since the mid-nineties, initially having to register with the State Environmental Protection Administration (SEPA). In addition, Chinese politics itself is not without individual, environmental champions. Ministerial level academics that raised environmental awareness include Qu Geping and Li Jinchang who co-authored the 1994 book "Population and the Environment in China".[58] Later, Zhang Yisheng and Qian Yihong co-authored "Grave Concerns: Problems of Sustainable Development in China" where China's fundamental problems of structure, corruption and state ownership are discussed and challenged.[59] As long as these individuals do not challenge the system or the party, they will be allowed to write, publish and criticize. The hope is that these small streams will form a big river.

Changing Structures

As aforementioned, there is a live and highly critical debate in China over the environment. In light of this, the Chinese media is reporting on the hundreds of events all across the country, such as people protesting against local pollution and environmental crime. The notion that the Chinese do not care about the environment, or that the environment is a luxury concern for the rich, is not correct. In fact, it is arguably the poor Chinese that care more in many aspects compared to the rich. While most of the internal debate and state criticism has been omitted in western media, the Chinese government is publicly criticizing itself, with the public and local media happy to join in.

Reinforcing the ability to criticize is the changing structure of families and traditional networks allowing people much greater positions of independence. The deconstruction of communal China and the gradual reform of the state's role in providing for families have meant that they have become more reliant on their own ability to fend for themselves. Farmers have been asked to leave the land, but not their region. They have been told to go to the factories in their area, but not to the city. Now they earn more, and the local government employs more while delivering targeted GDP growth.[60] The objectives set by Central Government are primed for growth, but not until recently for environmental sustainability as well. As the communes have been broken up there is only a small or non-existent safety network to fall back upon, other than that of one's own family. There is little guaranteed income at the end of the month, and food is not necessarily grown on one's own land.[61] As the economy is shifting from an entirely state-controlled economy to a largely private-owned economy, social and economic dynamics have changed.

A farmer depends on their plot of land to yield as much as possible to not go hungry, and to save for retirement and health costs. Thus, farmers are therefore more exposed to environmental degradation since their livelihood is at risk if their land is contaminated, flooded or dries up. The consequence of an environmental accident to a rural resident is therefore more serious. Then again, economic growth is equally likely to benefit their family through higher paid factory work or higher prices for their goods. Hence, pollution may be considered a tolerable cost in exchange for economic progress.

Environmental decay is of great concern for the rural, poor, farmers and migrant labor. It is the poor that typically need water from a river. It is the poor who cannot afford installing foreign air filters in their homes. It is the poor that cook with dirty coal stoves. It is the farmer that grows his produce next to a chemical plant. The poor cannot afford bottled water or imported tomatoes. It is the poor that cannot afford western cars with higher fuel standards and more expensive fuel.[62] So the poor may be the most affected by pollution, but also the least capable of escaping its consequences. On the other hand, the poor also have the most to benefit from economic progress, and are therefore much more likely to repress the cost of pollution. With the knowledge that they are also the ones most likely to benefit from economic progress, it is consequently probable that the poor will tolerate the costs of unhealthy water, air and food.

Not long ago, all environmental complaints would have gone to the heart of one's commune or state factory unit. A complaint would essentially hurt the very same organization providing one's food, income and housing. Thus, an enormous personal risk would be taken in lodging a complaint about pollution. In this way, economic reform and structural change in China actually enables the type of civilian action found in other countries.

Where people have direct economic benefits in the exploitation of nature, opposition will struggle to take roots. Opposition to the state, which provides greater global influence and improved economic status, will have unprecedented costs. If the state is criticized, the economic growth engine is jeopardized for everyone. As a consequence, it also seems far safer and productive to work for environmental protection within the state, rather than from the outside. Through working in the Ministry of Environmental Protection, or its sub-organizations, there is a mandate and ability to influence and make change. Or at least try. Conversely, working from inside the state can be slow and unsatisfactory, yet the near term solutions to China's most severe environmental challenges exist here. Since the Government has such a powerful grip on the economy, if the Leadership were to decide that environmental concerns are a priority on par or even above economic growth, then changes can be implemented quickly and comprehensively across the whole nation.

In other words, if President Xi decides to "clean things up," he and his environmentally inclined compatriots can make significant and rapid change. However, with an estimated 300 million people still living in relative poverty, focus remains on bringing the poor up the income curve, while encouraging sustainable practices among the state's economic agents. Until China has a more balanced economic distribution, the environment is likely to remain a lower priority compared to growth itself. While citizens are catching up economically, some degradation of the environment may be perceived as a tolerable cost, at least on a local level. However, certain pockets within the country are so rich and polluted, that they are literally choking. In these cities, cleaning up has started and must intensify in the next few years. For the local governments that have not caught up economically, they will be aware, yet repress the cost of economic growth even if they are the ones paying a disproportionate price. These structural changes in China are a byproduct of the rapid urbanization that the country has undergone in the last decades.

Urbanization

With "only" 600 million Chinese citizens currently living in cities, accounting for approximately 45% of the population, further rapid rural-urban migration can be expected.[1] If China were to approach western levels of urbanization, at about 80% of the population, more than 400 million people will migrate to the cities in the next decade or so. Most estimates predict approximately 1 billion Chinese will live in cities by 2025.[2] It is this continued urbanization, which will feed not only GDP growth, but also serious challenges related to water, land and energy demand. In 2011, the Chinese government announced that 20 new cities will be built each year over the next decade. China is expected to invest more than USD 15 trillion by the year 2030 in infrastructure alone.[3] To give a general idea of the investment breakdown, it is expected that about 40% of the investment will be in housing, 27% in water infrastructure, 16% on roads and railways, 13% on electricity networks, and the remainder in telecommunications, ports and airports.[4] The Central Government's own urbanization expectations indicate a 400% growth in GDP by 2020, where GDP generated by cities is expected to rise from 75% in 2009 to 95% in 2025. Urban consumption will contribute 33% of total GDP, or RMB 21.7 trillion, with aggregate consumption and disposable income double that of Germany's disposable income.[5]

In order to fuel urban consumption, 400-500 million urban jobs will be created, as China will account for 20% of global

GDP growth, 20% of global energy consumption and 25% of global oil demand. In terms of infrastructure, 170 cities are planned to meet mass-transit system planning criteria, double compared to Europe's current number. An additional 28,000 km of metro rail will be built to move urban citizens around.[6] Up until today, Chinese cities have grown more by geographical expansion than by migration itself. In fact, "expansionary tactics" are how many city governments have financed themselves up until today. City governments have appropriated more and more farmland, and sold it off for a profit to developers.[7] Land expropriation is a main cause of mass protests in China.[8] Selling land has provided the necessary capital for cities in building infrastructure, schools and hospitals. In the process it has also made many corrupt developers and government officials very rich.

There comes a point however, when most of the land has already been sold and city officials will struggle to find available farmland to expropriate. Future urbanization is more likely to come from migration rather than expansion as cities are simply running out of space. Land expropriation also tends to cause inflationary pressures when farmland disappears, food supply shrinks, with food inflation following. Food inflation infuriates consumers and makes governments anywhere concerned. Migrant workers arriving to Chinese cities experience a whole set of serious challenges. Unlike second-class citizens, they often have little entitlement to a number of social services available in the city. Social rights in China, including health care and schooling, are determined by a so-called *hukou,* or registration card held by all citizens. By definition, the migrant population does not have registration cards in the city, and correspondingly have few or no rights for social support in that location.[9] The Central Government has realized this social unfairness, and has begun several programs to provide migrant workers with basic healthcare and educational rights.[10] Although steps have been taken, there is much that still remains to provide equality of rights, independent of location, and such equality will take decades to implement.

China is aiming at developing different types of cities, from mid-sized to so-called "super-cities". Super-cities would include cities such as Beijing, Shanghai and Guangzhou with more than 20 million people each, and the mid-sized cities would range in size from a small to medium-sized European country. My home country of Norway, with a population just short of five million, would be the size of one of many small to mid-sized cities in China. Larger cities, much like companies, can benefit from the increased urbanization through economies of scale. Super-cities will be able to attract more talent, smarter technologies and higher-valued jobs. Companies located in super cities will meet higher competition and respond by hiring better people and employing newer technologies. Top branded universities will relocate to and expand in super cities; further driving innovation, competition and value creation. This combination is a positive cycle that lends itself well to super-cities and would not be enjoyed on the same scale if limits were placed on urbanization.

As urbanization unfolds, environmental benefits might be an unexpected externality. Super- and larger mid-sized cities are considerably more efficient when it comes to distributing electricity, in addition to people accepting working in smaller environments, which are easier to insulate or cool down. Jobs in cities are generally less electricity intensive, in the sense that IT businesses and financial service industries, for example, require much less energy than cement and steel production. Increased urban density can also reduce the amount of travel and vehicle use, assuming public transportation and infrastructure adequately match the scale of the city and its population. Cities will do what they can to attract, develop and retain a high-skill based population, be more productive and pollute less per capita. As cities attract more competent people, the population will also demand more from its government. A concentration of very competent and critical people in an urban environment may be good, but is also a ticking time bomb. While in this day and age a concentrated population may be easier to monitor, it will also present new challenges for city government officials not operating on the same wave length as its educated, well-travelled and sophisticated population.

Urban citizens will demand habitable centers and improved living standards. Cities should be prepared to "grow up, rather than out" and place new requirements on mass transportation. As Beijing is becoming increasingly congested, especially during peak hours, pollution levels can only be expected to worsen considerably, unless the car fleet is completely changed or materially upgraded. Studies estimate the car fleet in Shanghai alone to outstrip its road capacity by three-to-one, thus frequently shutting down the city and hurting its productivity, not to mention living standards. The urban sprawl will continue to strain the quantity of arable land available, declining ultimately to only 20% of the current arable land. Estimates place land space suitable for cultivation decreasing at a rate of 0.04 hectares for each new urban resident. Arable land per capita stood at a peak of 0.19 hectares per capita in 1965, but had dropped to 0.1 hectares per capita in 2003, followed by another 10% loss by 2010.[11] Government estimates are that by 2025, fertile land per capita may have fallen by 20-22%, aggravated by pollution, droughts and frequent floods.[12] Although China is ranked 11th globally for total amount of arable land suitable for wheat, maize, corn and rice, the country is ranked 175th in per capita terms. Chinese scientists have stated that increasing grain yields by 10% would not compensate for the impact on food production given the loss of arable land.[13] These statistics highlight the severity of China's current and future food production issues and shed light on China's eagerness to develop secure food supply elsewhere.

Since 1970, grain production in China has doubled and the annual compounded yield rate is now about 1.3%.[14] New technologies, grain types and machinery could drive yields upwards to 40-50% as China modernizes its agricultural industry. A serious obstacle to increased yields is access to water, with urban water demand expected to increase by 65-100% in the next 5-10 years. Southern China has 400% more water per capita compared to northern China, thus making the geographic distribution of water sources a great challenge. To put the water situation in perspective, China's total resources are similar to American levels. Yet, on a per capita basis this brings China's supplies to only one-third of America's. From 2003 to 2005, the average usage per capita in China was about 375 cubic meters of water annually, compared to 1,730 cubic meters in the US.[15] Chinese per capita growth lied around 3% annually, with urban residents using 211 liters daily, compared to rural residents using only 68 liters per day. Having said that, 70% of water use in China was for agricultural purposes, with only 13% used by residential consumers. Residential water use grows much faster though, doubling every 10 years. The northern cities, such as Beijing and Tianjin, are forecasted to exceed sustainable local water supplies in the next 5-10 years.[16] The water shortage could worsen if usage is not curtailed.

Fortunately, some measures can be taken in order to reduce water consumption or improve usage efficiency. It is estimated that more than 40% of urban water demand could be reduced if water-saving measures and leakages are addressed. Also, the water tariff in China is deemed to be much too low, especially in northern cities, which permits excessive use due to the low costs. For example, urban residents' water costs are estimated at 0.48% of total income, compared to 1.5% in France.[17] China should rapidly increase its water tariffs to address the shortage by discouraging pricier water use. At the very least, water prices should increase as much as inflation or average urban wage increases. Also, the Government could relatively easily require all new toilets sold to be "water efficient toilets", which industry estimates say could lead to a total of 20% reduction in water usage. Likewise, a requirement for industry to only sell "water efficient shower heads" and "water efficient washing machines" could lead to another 30% reduction in consumption.[18] There are new technologies, which can be employed easily if the political will existed. Let us hope these little streams literally will form a big river.

Every province and city in China are different and in fierce competition with each other. Indeed, the politicians themselves are in fierce competition with each other, if not even in a literal battle of life and death as the so-called "Bo Xilai" case in 2012 so publically displayed. It is very easy to underestimate the level of competition between mayors and governors in China. The political promotion cycle is still mainly based on achieving economic targets, and officials are not always accountable to pay back debts after the political cycle has run its turn.[19] These traits result in vastly different and conflicting executions of government policies in the cities. Cities in China, either naturally or by policy implementation, seem to specialize and develop comparative advantages through hubs and spikes. As examples, Tianjin is focused on an expertise in logistics and financial services, while Hangzhou is developing its expertise in IT and e-commerce. With cities developing competitive strengths, people and companies will also need to adapt the particular "strategies" on where to live or where to establish a foothold. A "one size fits all" approach to China is less likely to be successful given the varying stages of development and consumer preferences.

Rapid urbanization and migration labor has resulted in some "creative" solutions to housing demand. As cities rapidly develop, cheaper housing is often replaced by expensive apartments, with no cheap substitutes provided. Clearing temporary "villages within cities" has caused a surge in alternative lodging, which migrant workers can afford.[20] Government surveys indicate that approximately 130 million migrant workers live in improvised spaces, where small areas are further sub-divided and then rented out.[21] For example, in Shanghai, migrant workers live in old shipping containers that have been refurbished in response to a shortage of affordable housing.

These so-called "container villages" and other temporary lodgings raise critical issues concerning China's urbanization. The Government does not allow these temporary housing quarters, and work tirelessly to shut them down. At the same time, new housing is not affordable enough for residents of such temporary lodgings, creating a net loss of housing units.

The affordable housing created is too expensive for people to buy or rent; yet shanty towns are not permitted either. After photos of the Shanghai container villages surfaced on the Internet, the government proceeded to clamp down on this form of housing.[22] In a cruel twist of fate, local officials pointed out that the former farmland is now urban, and the migrant workers must move while the site is "remodeled" for commercial use.[23] As housing costs in China increase, finding appropriate living space in general becomes more difficult by the day.

In 2008, I managed to buy a house in Beijing where we have lived since. Today, five years later, it is ready for renovation. When buying a new house in China, you essentially get a concrete shell, with the exterior being the only finished element. You are expected to do all of the interior decorating, from basic plumbing, to installing the kitchen and bathrooms, and installing the electrical wiring. As mentioned, the house now looks ready for a renovation job, mainly because of the relatively poor and cheap building materials available. All my neighbors seem to have similar situations. General upgrading and renovation seems to account for a considerably higher proportion of investment and disposable income here, significantly higher than one would expect from Europe or the US. It is easy to imagine that the unnecessary waste from cheap building materials and five-year time loops of renovations are not efficient, nor particularly great for the environment. Yet, it does stimulate consumption as people trade accommodation and style upwards. I cannot decide if it is a good thing that the old shipping containers west of my living compound are now gone and Orwellian apartment blocks are stretching up and out.

There is a significant possibility that the West, and China itself, underestimates the growth and resources needed to deliver the projected Chinese growth. By 2030, China could have approximately 1 billion urban residents. The consulting company McKinsey famously predicted that China could build 170 mass-transit systems, 40 billion square meters of floor space, five billion square meters of road and 15 megacities with populations above 25 million before 2020.[24] The Chinese GDP may multiply five times to about USD 25 trillion in the next 10-15 years. As much as I am excited about the investment opportunities in clean technologies for the next decade, I am also convinced that the Chinese consumer market has obvious financial dangers. As in any "ocean of opportunity" there are deceptive rocks and bubbles that will burst. An aging population, for example, may both be a blessing and a curse.

City Tiers and Changing Demographics

The last decade of GDP growth in China is partly credited to urbanization at home and exports abroad, fueled by a bulging working population. Simple population growth has provided a demographic dividend for China. This workforce has now peaked and growth will not continue as easily. In 2012 alone, the Chinese labor force declined by 3.45 million people, leaving the labor force base at 937 million, according to the National Bureau of Statistics (NBS).[25] Similarly, the United Nations forecasts working population between the age of 15 and 59 to drop by about 24 million people by year 2025.[26] At the same time, the age group above 65 years old will *increase* by about 65 million, opening up many challenges and opportunities alike in health and pharmaceutical industries.[27]

A widely followed Chinese demographer, Cai Fang, has long argued that the Chinese workforce has peaked. As head of the Chinese Academy of Social Sciences' Institute of Population and Labor Economics, Cai stated in 2013 that the "surplus labor pool is diminishing".[28] This comment was made in context of Apple Computer's supplier Foxconn having shifted production from its early base in the coastal regions to new manufacturing sites in the inland areas of Henan, Sichuan and Chongqing.[29] Migrant workers previously working in Beijing and Shanghai are now moving back to their original provinces to settle down and work. A combination of new well-paying jobs, cheaper real estate and convenient local residence permits are attracting them back home. The wage differences between coastal and western provinces are declining, and will eventually converge. The pursuit of cheap labor costs in China is getting harder and cost leadership has actually already been conceded to South East Asian countries like Vietnam, the

Philippines and Indonesia.[30]

Uneven geographical population distribution may contribute to an irregular growth trajectory in years to come. Inland migration is expected to fuel the development in western provinces, spreading economic growth there, with western areas seeing higher growth rates than more developed areas.[31] Varying population sizes and levels of economic development have led to a distinction of city tiers in China. The difference between these so-called first- and lower-tier cities in China is important to note. First-tier cities are commonly agreed to be Beijing in the north, Shanghai on the coast, and Shenzhen and Guangzhou in the south. Definitions for second- and third-tier cities are somewhat vague, but generally include the 23 secondary provincial capitals and prefecture- or county-level capitals as well. There is an undefined number of third-tier cities, with potentially over 100 of these cities depending on the definitions used. These cities all have populations above one million, and are still growing. Cities viewed as second-tier cities include central cities like Chongqing and Chengdu, along with Tianjin on the northern coast. Despite the various definitions, the differences between the tiers stretch from the amount of skilled labor or services available, infrastructure, potential for growth to competition for deals and management quality.

In the cases of skilled labor, services and infrastructure, the degree of availability in various tier cities is noticeably dissimilar. First-tier cities have typically benefitted from decades of investment, and are consequently much more developed than lower-tier cities. This development translates into a larger pool of skilled workers, due to the proximity of universities and attractive higher wages. Services will consequently center on these highly developed areas, along with the infrastructure created from previous developments. Second- and third-tier cities suffer from opposite issues, where lower levels of development results in a lack of skilled labor, with youths often developing an attraction to the first-tier cities. Second- and third-tier cities are often removed from the coast and typically lack in infrastructure.[32] This rural-urban migration beginning from a young age causes a "brain drain", which exacerbates the lack of development in less developed areas.

Conducting business in a first- versus second- or third-tier city has many distinctions. Since first-tier cities have already developed comparatively more, the growth potential may be lower and wages and real estate costs are higher. Lower-tier cities on the other hand, still have plenty of room for growth, further facilitated by comparatively low production and real estate costs. Similarly, because fewer professional investors reside in second tier cities, there is less competition for deals, thus providing an opening for investors into high growth sub-territories. Foreign investors and businesses alike would be well advised to consider an inland move, especially in the face of a growing consumer base in second- and third-tier cities.

Although consumers in first-tier cities tend to have higher levels of income, the consumer base as a whole is significantly larger in second- and third-tier cities. Back of the envelope calculations indicate that the first-tier city population ranges between 60 to 65 million. Using similar definitions, second- and third-tier cities' total population ranges from 400 to 750 million people. Regardless of which "city definition" is used, the number of consumers in lower-tier cities is significantly higher than the tier-one cities. While input costs and salaries are rising in the second- and third-tier cities, this also will create higher disposable income and higher consumption there. Henan province is China's most populous province with more than 100 million people and is also home to three of the fastest-growing Chinese cities, namely Zhengzhou, Jiaozhuo and Xinxiang. In Zhengzhou, the surge in employment opportunities resulted in almost 3 million new residents from the countryside over the last few years. By 2020, the number of urban residents in Zhengzhou receiving annual wages of RMB 75,000 (USD 12,500) is expected to double that of Shanghai.[33]

In 2009, I invested in a lithium ion battery maker in Henan province, not so much to take advantage of labor costs, but because there was a cluster of battery companies in the city of Xinxiang. The city is twice the population size of Oslo, the capital of Norway, yet is only the third or fourth largest city in Henan province. The reason battery companies had blossomed in this region, and in this city in particular, was that Chairman Mao decided back in the 1960s that the local military forces were to move into mountainous caves outside the city in case of a nuclear war. To survive in the mountains or in the caves, the military would require batteries to operate its equipment. Hence, a large and vibrant battery business developed in the cities around these mountains and the military industry there. Of the more than 200 battery companies that are reported to exist in Xinxiang City, I have invested in one of them. In the last three years – salaries have risen about 60% in the city, an extraordinary amount. However, since the wage increase is from a low base, the rise has not nearly removed the price competitiveness relative to the USA, where much of the international competition originates.

Given that second- and third-tier cities have more reasonably priced real estate, this reduced cost frees up higher spending capabilities for local consumers. The "rising tide lifts all boats" bodes well for an overall rise in Chinese consumption. The young generation has not seen the Cultural Revolution or the horrid past of China, consequently the so-called 'post-1980s' generation of Chinese youth have a 'spend it if you've got it' attitude, contributing strongly to a rise in consumer spending. As once-poor provinces develop, the composition of consumption in its role to stimulate economic growth will be reshaped. The increase in disposable income coincides with the changing consumption psychology among the youth, where brands are perceived as investments reflective of social status.[34]

Domestic and foreign companies have already picked up on the emerging consumer pool in lower-tier cities. Brands such as cosmetics company L'Oreal, sportswear maker Adidas, coffee chain Starbucks and car manufacturer General Motors (GM) have already established a new strategic focus on lower tier cities in China. L'Oreal predicts the middle class to expand by 260 million people by 2020 and the company recently stated "Tier three cities are really important for us. They're growing really fast and are a way for us to reach the Chinese soaring middle class".[35] Adidas plans to double its presence in lower tier cities in the next two years, with the intention to expand to 1,400 cities across China by 2015. Starbucks also aims to increase the number of stores beyond first-tier cities by 20-30% in the next few years: while GM intends to triple its sales of luxury brand Cadillac by 2015 through targeting smaller cities. GM said at the Shanghai Auto Show in 2013 that "the tier-one cities' market is large, but the market is getting saturated. But tier-two and tier-three, there's high potential for growth."[36]

Against a demographic headwind, the rate of economic expansion will be driven by the desire of Chinese citizens to improve their quality of life. In order to offset a declining population, measures from Chinese bureaucrats like abolishing the "one child policy" are to be expected. Responsible for the creation of "little emperors" who become the sole focus of not only their parents, but also their grandparents, the one child policy is overdue for reform. Changing the policy will have an effect, but will obviously be limited in its initial impact on growth and global competitiveness. Yet, changing such a monumental policy is a potent tool that policy-makers can invoke with a simple signature on a paper. No other economies in the world have similar options for stimulating growth, providing China with some ready-made policy options and flexibilities, which could have a great impact on future growth. While consumption is on the rise and the service sector is gaining GDP significance, fixed asset investments and improvements in basic infrastructure, such as communication, transport, water irrigation or energy transmission are likely to outweigh the slowing of rural families moving into urban dwellings.

The Chinese government gave the world a sneak peak of a "master plan" on how to convert old industrial townships into modern cities when the new "Urban Regeneration Plan" was launched in 2013. The plan sets out the actions and investments needed from 2013 through to 2020 in order to convert 95 "industry heavy" cities and 25 municipalities into sustainable service economic zones.[37] These former industrial areas will receive government funding to invest in technology, housing and infrastructure, in addition to the necessary financial support for the people laid off from large State Owned Enterprises (SOEs). The Urban Regeneration Plan intends for these ex-industrial cities to create nearly 20% of local GDP from high technology industries. Services' contribution is targeted to account for 45% of the local economy, a level services has already reached in the broader economy. The plan includes several ambitious environmental goals as well: water consumption per unit of industrial output is expected to be reduced to 32% of the levels in 2012 and energy consumption per unit of local GDP to fall by 18%. The plan estimates that the investment provided alone will increase residents' annual disposable income per capita by RMB 29,000 (about USD 5,000), along with more than 13 million new jobs expected to be created in the process.[38]

The Urban Regeneration Plan is exactly the type of step that the Government must take. It is likely that they will not succeed everywhere, and inevitable fiascos will be widely covered in the media. Almost as a side effect, China stands the chance of developing particularly advanced and world-leading industries as a consequence of the existing research and development in combination with the large scale of the home market. China is in a position to take global leadership in fields such as advanced materials technologies, energy efficiency and conservation, biotechnology, clean energy vehicles and the whole information technology value chain. President Xi seems to believe that the Chinese economy must shift away from an investment driven export model towards domestic consumption and services, a view shared by most environmentalists in China.

The Housing Market

The housing market in China has been a one-direction play in recent years. Despite Government efforts to cool down the property market, its rise seems almost unstoppable. Citizens not able to enter the property market tend to become very angry and frustrated, making property one of the most potent social and economic risk factors in China. Equally, the possibility of a sudden drop in property prices will be a serious challenge to the country's stability. A new set of curbs seem to be unleashed on the property market every quarter or so with the latest being a 20% capital gain tax on property sales and the strictest price control rules in urban markets to date. Limits on how much property prices can rise were set through linking allowable house price increases to per capita disposable income growth rates. Down-payment requirements and interest rates for second-home purchase loans were both increased and these measures are expected to be further tightened in the next years.[39]

Currently, there is a ban on single-person households to purchase a second residence.[40] Stop for a minute to consider that restriction. Can you mention any country around the world where that is a restriction? Is not that an amazing fact in itself? The government is essentially saying: "You cannot buy more properties now. That's it. One property is enough for you!" Simply restricting demand is not going to solve the overheating of the house market in China. Limiting demand must be complemented by a generous supply of affordable housing. The UK, France and the US all had similar housing projects in the 1950s, 1960s and a few in the 1970s as well. That period is where China currently is in terms of urbanization. The Government plans to spend more than USD

6 trillion on affordable housing and related infrastructure in the next 10 years.[41] History tells us that the bulk of this construction may not win environmental or design awards, and could cause a net reduction of housing as migrant dwellings are removed, with the aim to send workers back to their home cities or home provinces.

In my neighborhood in Beijing, there are many smaller "Hutong" villages around the larger apartment blocks. These villages are where maids and construction workers live, both local and migrant workers. The buildings are essentially supplied with electricity, but there is no proper heating, nor sanitation. Those who need to use the bathroom in the middle of the night, must get up, get dressed, and walk down the street to the public toilet. This toilet is nothing compared to what western individuals would find clean or accommodating. It does not matter if you are five or 80 years old, or if it is summer or winter, if you need to "go" you need to get up, get dressed and go down the street to the public toilet. It is not a very pleasant experience. Heating is coal-fired and while summer life on the streets has a certain charm to both locals and foreigners living in the area, it holds a lot less charm for the ones stuck in the middle of it. A lot of foreigners, especially tourists that visit, seem to think it is a "shame that the old ways of Beijing life are disappearing." This view is most definitely not shared by the bulk of people living there every day. They want to move to a small apartment with a modern kitchen, central heating, water and a separate water closet. The villagers expand their houses as much as they can, partly because any extra rooms are rented out to the temporary workers for about RMB 500 (USD 85) per month, but also because the more square meters they have, the more compensation may be received if the land is eventually expropriated. As the village is demolished and replaced by yet another apartment building, migrant workers will likely move on to the next village in an endless game, and the locals will trade up to a small apartment with modern facilities.

Chinese media have dubbed the new middle class of urban Chinese entering the property market as "Fang Nu" or "Housing Slaves" since 30-50% of their disposable income is spent to repay mortgages.[42] A 100 square meter apartment in Beijing or Shanghai now costs approximately 40 years of average income for a single person. As a general rule, banks assess payment capacity at 50% of disposable income with down payment now ranging from 30-40%. Mortgages to private people for housing are only about 20% of the typical Chinese bank's total lending, so the private property sector in China is largely equity financed and not a systemic, economic risk.

Chinese citizens expect that housing prices in first tier cities will continue to grow significantly in the next 10 years and beyond. Required down payment on first mortgages rose from 20% to 30% in 2012 and there is a whopping 60% minimum deposit for second-home purchases, while second loan interest rates are on the rise.[43] Property taxes initially imposed only in Shanghai and Chongqing have now spread nationwide and more restrictions and property curbs are expected in the years to come. These property taxes can seem apt when in January 2013 alone, there was over a 1% increase in new home prices in China, which corresponds to the largest gain in two years. The average sales price per square meter reached USD 1,577 in 100 Chinese cities in 2013.[44]

The private property ownership reforms were started by the

former Prime Minister Zhu Rongji in 1998.[45] Through privatizing state-owned housing by transferring home ownership from the state to the families living in the houses themselves, these reforms have been an amazing success. Up to 250 million people have received property from the Chinese state, whose individual net wealth has increased phenomenally in the last 15 years of urbanization. The sharp rise in property value has more than offset the increased interest rates and inflation. Between 50-70% of home buyers in Shanghai, Beijing and Guangzhou have in addition borrowed at an average of 50% of their initial state-provided home value to buy new and improved apartments.[46] This has created an inflated level of demand, where people outside of the cities have found it more expensive and difficult to enter the property market. If you happened to live and work in a city, you won the big property lottery ticket, but correspondingly, if you lived and worked outside the city, you may have been hopelessly sidelined.

The cheap housing that migrant workers have found in Chinese cities has participated in keeping labor costs low in China. It is unthinkable that the government could have provided housing to all the migrant workers around China, yet they have found cheap temporary residences. It is estimated that nearly half of migrant workers live in dormitories provided by their employers, and the others live in makeshift or cheap privately rented housing arrangements.[47] These temporary dwellings have contributed in large part to keeping labor costs down and China cost competitive with the rest of Asia. It is also highly unlikely that the migrant housing market is fully accounted for in the official GDP figures, suggesting that Chinese GDP figures could be significantly larger than the official figures. The scale of the unofficial or so-called "black" economy is not to be taken lightly, because as the unofficial economy is brought in line with the official economy, GDP numbers are expected to increase. Some economic estimates set the unofficial Chinese economy at about half the size of the official economy, pegging current total GDP estimates at around USD 12 trillion.[48] Whatever the size, the Beijing City government estimated that there were almost 300 temporary and unofficial villages within the city in 2010, but only about 100 remained as of 2012 due to "cleaning up" policies.[49] As these villages disappear, affordable housing will be under pressure to expand and property prices will be underpinned.

An area of some, but not general economic concern, is the so-called ghost towns found in many places of China. These are development projects that were initiated and consequently partly, or fully, completed, without being sold or having anyone actually moving into them. Many "Armageddon is coming" articles have been written from various ghost cities, including Inner Mongolia's Ordos region where the Kangbashi "ghost city" is located.[50] With local city governments and developers both overly optimistic and greedy, a mismatch has occurred between certain locations that are overheating and others that will never be sold. Property developments in China have not been perfect and many will suffer in terms of their financial return, but it is better to have invested in housing and basic infrastructure than in consumer goods manufacturing over-capacity. It seems that the first tier cities have deep and broad demand with little or no oversupply, while the situation is different in more remote provinces. Developers and local governments are gambling that these areas will fill up over the next years or decade; some will not.

City Transportation

If cities are to be habitable, they need to invest in mass transportation to reduce travel times and polluting congestion. The Civil Aviation Administration of China (CAAC) is planning to construct 82 additional airports by 2015 in a plan to increase the Chinese airport network by about 50%. The airports would become major local hubs allowing for easy transport within all regions of China. Many Chinese feel the country should develop more rail networks instead, because Chinese airlines and airports are already struggling to survive, not to mention that air traffic pollutes more than railway travel. Additionally, more than 75% of China's airports are reported to be in deficit and chances of the situation improving in the future are bleak.[51] While China has only 180 regional airports, Brazil has 700 and the US has 19,000. This contrast is more a reflection of the number of small and local airports in Brazil and the US for private aviation. This comparison is misconstrued, as there is no private aviation industry to speak of in China, so the real comparisons are in fact the larger airports and air traffic numbers. In 2011, China had 53 airports each serving over 1 million passengers while Brazil only had 28. The same year, 43 Chinese airports independently handled over 2 million passengers, while the US had 62.[52] Despite the US having served more passengers, the similarities in air traffic began to show. Furthermore, America's largest airport, Atlanta, boards only half as many passengers compared to Beijing. Part of the challenge in China is that every local municipality and city wants their own airport, mainly driven by a desire to stimulate local economic growth. Locally it might be good politics, but holistically and environmentally it does not seem equally sound.

Luckily, China's Central Government appears fixated on high-speed railways with China already having the world's largest high-speed network at 9,000 km, with a goal to expand it to 16,000 kilometers by 2020.[53] Not unaccustomed to mega projects, construction on the Beijing-Guangzhou rail line started in 2002 and was only completed in 2012. Railway transportation emits significantly less carbon emissions and pollution compared to flying, thus the development is also beneficial to the environment. Similar to electric vehicles, however, high-speed rails require electricity, predominantly created by coal-fired power plants. Thus, this low-emission transportation system is still being fueled by an emission-intensive power source. That said, railways "mainly" require electricity, not the liquid kerosene used by airplanes, thus reducing China's dependency on foreign oil, along with all the related price and supply volatilities. It seems in China's interest to further build intercity rail and high-speed rail transportation, rather than building land-intensive airports for every municipality.

As China prepares to house more than 300 million people in cities, local Communist Party officials say that they are intent on planning and building a whole new United States of America in 10-15 years. It is a powerful analogy. China plans to build all the towns and cities for 300 million people with the infrastructure to connect and operate them. The price tag for that project will be 10 times greater than the current US GDP, a daunting, but absolutely wonderful challenge. Imagine the opportunity to partake in the building of one entire America over a short period in your career? That prospect should make local politicians excited. Businesses all over the world are excited as well, but the environment maybe not so much. The trillion-dollar question is how does China avoid making the mistakes of western urbanization? How does one avoid social division, downtown areas without life after 6 p.m. or ghetto-like environments altogether? How does one speed build a harmonious society on a budget that runs on a schedule?

The very first aspect of a Chinese middle-class lifestyle that must be changed is the fascination with and need for the automobile. This trend has not started off well, with current city infrastructure focused on a massive highway and city ring-road transport systems with giant apartment blocks stacked in between. 2012 was a record year for the Chinese automotive sector in terms of sales. Total vehicle population reached 240 million, including 120 million passenger cars.[54] That same year also saw 15 million new cars added onto the streets with car ownership exceeding 1 million in 18 Chinese cities. New automobile sales are expected to reach 20 million in 2013 as China's economy keeps rebalancing. The increased number of passenger vehicles will sadly dampen efforts to improve environmental quality.

Carbon emissions and gigantic productivity losses from standstills on the highway will only be the tip of the iceberg. American and most European suburbs are built with people living in villas or three-four story apartment blocks. In China those blocks are 10 stories high on average. It is simply not possible to transport people by car to work or for social commutes at those urban living densities. Urban city planners seem slow to recognize this fact. Some of the ghost cities built around China make evident that the Government is trying to distribute urbanization more evenly as it is obviously not possible for 1.3 billion people to live in Beijing and Shanghai. These cities must be built and eventually filled. China needs to return to the memories I have of *hutongs* and local neighborhoods. City planners need to build cities and suburbs where people can still walk to work, or hop on their bicycle to see friends. People need to be able to take a short bus ride to their destination, or go out to local shops and restaurants to consume. Whereas much of the debate remains on how to secure enough natural resources and reduce the environmental consequences, the dialogue now also needs to include sociological objectives. How do we want to live? Will we be happy in giant apartment blocks? Is that the lifestyle we want for our children and grandchildren? I am not witnessing a vibrant debate over these issues in the Chinese media, nor among planners and politicians.

As long as the car is a symbol of success and elevated status to the middle class, China is in trouble. Coupled with a strong intent from the domestic automobile industry to expand, the road ahead looks quite challenging. City planning in China is made more problematic by local governments who need to sell land to developers to finance local services. Developers aim to sell as many square meters per acre of land, and hence are intending to build large, skyscraper-like apartment blocks with less consideration for transportation, working hubs and green, livable environments. Breaking down the land plots to allow various types of living environments and offices are the role and responsibility of the country's mayors and governors. So long as these officials are measured against their achieved GDP growth and the absence of political scandals, China will not succeed. A much broader set of human and social objectives must be incorporated in the political promotion system for China's cities to become livable.

Social issues are intertwined here as well. Historically speaking, in countries where the urbanization rate reaches

50%, material increases in tension levels have been observed.[55] As discussed earlier, most social incidents have related to land disputes, foreign incidents or local corruption and unfairness. However, when people walked out on the streets in January 2013 protesting against how Beijing had injected an editorial in a local Guangzhou newspaper without consent from the local editor; it was one of the first episodes where Chinese people were not simply protesting a land issue or policy that directly impacted them.[56] Going out to protest for the right of editorial freedom has no immediate self-interest. It puts the individuals at risk and many who came to the paper's headquarters to show support for the cause were removed from the premises. This development is quite recent and indicates a selflessness, which Chinese authorities may have to adjust to, but which is an inevitable consequence of urbanization.

Chinese Consumption

Chinese consumption is strongly dependent on young consumers and the urban settling down of migrant workers. President Xi's Chinese Dream of changed consumption patterns is expected to play a pivotal role in China's structural shift away from an industrial, export driven economy to domestic services and a sustainable future. Chinese coastal cities account for an estimated 35% of all consumption in China today, with an international high household savings rate of 28% of disposable income.[57] A limited social safety system is seen as the major impediment for releasing consumption, placing focus on both improving the safety net as well as increasing income. As disposable income grows, so does consumption, as there is simply more money to go around. Both disposable and total incomes have increased at record paces in the last few years, averaging 30% growth since 2010.[58]

General Motors (GM) intends to triple the sales of its luxury Cadillac car by 2015 in China. In order to do this, GM aims to increase its dealerships in China from about 100 in 2013 to more than 200 in 2015.[59] This target will be met by focusing on second- and third-tier cities, where GM has stated the markets are less saturated. The consulting company McKinsey and Company expects the luxury car market alone to sell about 3 million units in 2020. In 2012, Cadillac sold about 30,000 units in China, but have plans to sell over 100,000 in 2015. By comparison, Audi sold about 405,000 units, BMW sold 327,000 and Mercedes-Benz sold about 200,000 units in the same year.[60] While these statistics are impressive, China's growing consumerism needs to be examined a bit more closely beyond the hopes of western companies.

A decreasing labor force with increasing wages, referred to by economists as the Lewis Turning Point, signals that China can no longer rely on its previous strength of manufacturing. China urgently needs to meet its loss in cost competitiveness with increased productivity and a shift to human capital that can be employed in a greener, more value added service economy. At the same time, consumption must be stimulated. In 2012, the service industry held the largest proportion of total employment in China, at about 36% of the total, with agriculture at 35% and manufacturing at 29%.[61] By comparison, service jobs in Russia and Brazil in 2009 constituted about 60% and 80% of the workforce respectively. South Korea and Japan both went from about 30% of work force in the service industry around 1960 to accounting for more than 60% each three decades later.[62] South Korea and Japan had their own Lewis Turning Point in the 1980s. In China, we should expect a similar, but faster development. Information and software services saw new job openings in 2012 rising over 30%, largely driven by the private sector.[63]

A general concern in China is that official data is seldom accurate. While China is likely to overstate their GDP growth figures, there are suggestions that Chinese consumption could be undervalued by as much as USD 1.6 trillion.[64] Official data reported that private consumption only constituted roughly 35% of GDP in 2012, but the economists at the global investment bank Morgan Stanley estimate Chinese consumption to account for 46% of GDP in 2012, up from 37% in 2008. These huge differences are explained by the absence of specific sectors such as financial services, health care, housing data and e-commerce. The exclusion of online purchases on websites such as Taobao is particularly interesting, considering how widespread Internet shopping is in general in China. If major online industries, such as most e-commerce and online gaming, are not fully included in Government statistics, then it is very probable that China's GDP figures are under-reported. There are two fascinating statistics in support of this premise: First, on November 11, 2012, better known as "Singles' Day" in China, USD 3 billion was spent on two Chinese online shopping sites alone: Taobao and Tmall.[65] Second, the Chinese online gaming industry earned about USD 10 billion in revenues in 2012. As consumer habits change, so too must the approach we take to measure the economy, especially here in China.

In general, Chinese government statistics should be doubted. Already in 2006, the Organization for Economic Co-operation and Development (OECD) simply stated the national accounts for China were "wrong", because figures were framed within a set of predetermined targets. The next year, now-prime minister Li Keqiang commented the output figures for Liaoning province, which he was party chief of at the time, were "man-made" and "for reference only".[66] Premier Li noted the discrepancies after the data was compared with other growth indicators, such as rail cargo volumes, bank lending and electricity consumption. These indicators are well-worth keeping in mind if growth statistics seem either too optimistic, or surprisingly low. Another statistic, which I find difficult to believe, is the official rural-urban income gap figure. It is entirely unlikely that farmers, or urban dwellers for that matter, really submit all their income to the tax authorities. The gap is estimated to be exaggerated by up to 40% according to the Chinese Academy of Social Sciences, and supports my earlier comments on the size of the unofficial economy in China.[67] Whatever the size and cleanliness of consumption might be compared to the manufacturing and industry, the progression to where we are today has clearly had a multifaceted impact on the environment.

Chinese consumers and companies alike are "happily" unaware of their carbon footprints and have a generally poor understanding of carbon audits and their impact on the environment. Generally, Chinese companies will approach decisions with a cost-benefit analysis, including pollution fees and reputational costs. For example, water treatment of polluted or contaminated water costs about USD 0.1-0.2 per metric ton.[68] It follows that companies using water in its production process can save money by simply dropping polluted water into the sewer systems untreated. Especially the textile industry which uses a lot of water for its processes continue to be seen as a prime polluter of water with heavy metals, carcinogens, and organic material that remove oxygen from rivers. A relatively recent Chinese crackdown on textile factories showed dye contamination levels of wastewater were at 19.5 times the legal limit.[69] As long as fines for environmental crimes are minuscule compared to cost savings from treatment, people and companies will "keep flushing".

China has become a net importer of electronic waste like printers, computers, television sets and other electric appliances. Electronic waste is growing at triple the rate of most other waste as the lifespans of technological gadgets are shortening and demand for consumer electronics is growing. In 1998, 20 million computers were "recycled" in the US. By 2009, this figure had grown to nearly 50 million computers.[70] In 2011, China alone discarded more than 160 million electronic appliances. Electronic waste is set to more than double in the next 10 years with poorer countries being the prime destination for electronic waste recycling. In Guiyu city in China's south, more than 100,000 people work in electronic waste recycling. Plastics and circuit boards are separated through boiling, and then metals are leached with acid in processes carried out in small backyard operations. Fumes are inhaled and fluids are flushed straight into the sewer or into the ground with local miscarriage rates skyrocketing.[71] As western countries are keen to outsource their waste recycling to poorer areas in China or other places, there is always a local mayor or businessman that stands ready to take on the opportunity, in the process creating local growth and jobs.

When I first moved my family to China in 1997, we spent the first nights in Beijing at Kunlun Hotel, one of the many unusual business extensions of the Chinese People's Liberation Army. Finding an apartment was a priority with a six-week old baby whom we were not entirely sure should be in Beijing in the first place. Having settled in the Shunyi area near the Beijing Capital Airport, a westernized lifestyle was shamelessly easy to adopt with the additional luxuries of a local *ayi* and a "market" around every corner. Used to the idea of recycling waste after having lived in Chicago and Oslo, we started looking for ways to recycle our garbage. Our maid from Hunan found the idea of recycling entirely comical and simply refused the idea of separating our garbage on location. *"Don't worry"*, she said; *"I will first take whatever I think is of value from your garbage, and then the rest will be recycled or eaten by someone."* The fact that my garbage will be fine-combed by several people looking for value has made me somewhat more conscious of what I am putting into the garbage to this day, but also more reckless since "someone else is going to do the job". I have tried to follow our garbage's post-Rynning household life. After the maid has taken what she wants, which is mainly bottles and plastic containers, the rubbish is taken outside the gated community, where the garbage is separated by hand. Nothing is missed. Paper, plastic, metal, and food are all recycled, made possible by cheap labor. The "someone" eating our organic waste is hopefully some fairly happy pigs in the not too far away neighborhood. It is possible that this is effective, but evidence suggests the "system" cannot cope with the 13,000 metric tons of garbage that the city of Beijing produces – every day.[72] According to local officials in Beijing, the current landfills and waste treatment plants are already stretched to capacity.[73] Particularly nasty toxins can leak into the ground water, thus I have for some time been looking at finding investment opportunities in the waste treatment sectors in China. Chinese regulations on filtering and collecting leakage from waste treatment plants are some of the most rigorous in the world, but enforcement seems weak. While disposal of mercury, dioxin and cadmium are not permitted; they are also largely not measured and monitored, especially in second- and third-tier cities.

Dumping of industrial waste does create thousands of "social incidents" or protests in China every year. We are talking about citizens gathering at city halls, or public sites all over the country. Almost all of them have one thing in common: they are not calling for the communist party to relinquish power. They ask to be heard when it comes to particular environmental problems. For example, near Beijing's Haidian District there were massive protests in 2012 regarding the so-called Liulitun landfill.[74] After media picked up on the story, a number of local officials were charged and imprisoned subsequent the discoveries following the protests. China has no lack of land. It is the fifth largest country of the world in terms of landmass. Thus, local governments have responded by pushing polluting industry, toxic waste plants or landfills further and further away from the cities. It does help some in terms of improving the immediate dangers of inhaling toxic air, but it does not solve the fundamental problems of waste disposal and polluting industries. Furthermore, toxic air travels, not only in China but also to neighboring countries. Japan[75] and South Korea[76] can measure significantly higher pollution levels when the wind blows from China towards their respective countries. Pollution knows no borders.

Anthropology professor Judith Shapiro has in a brilliant and sad way described China's "cancer villages" in her many books, including the gradual trend of cancer villages moving westwards, along with companies in pursuit of land and cheaper operating costs. Shapiro refers to "cancer clusters" and more than 459 cancer villages are identified by China Central Television, the Communist Party controlled state media.[77] Cancer villages are not a state secret, with even the Chinese state media reporting and writing about them. The cancer villages are defined as especially grotesque cases where whole families have cancer and the frequency and probability of developing cancer are off the scales. Shapiro writes that in a village she has followed called Huangmengying, with a small population of 2,400 people, one saw more than half of all deaths being caused by cancer, with 80% of the young people being constantly ill.[78] The death rate of the city is higher than the birth rate, and villagers are heavily in debt because of the medical bills. Shapiro concludes that these villagers are also at a huge disadvantage to stand up to businesses and local officials because they are poor, illiterate and not well organized. They are also sick and probably exhausted. Most of them will probably die there, having had their life quality and life expectancy greatly reduced for the benefit of urban dwellers.

White Knights in Electric Cars

At the risk of being overconfident, I maintain faith in the emerging Chinese middle class consumers shifting focus and demand for safer food, water and air. Actually, faith is not needed, as is demonstrated by the so-called environmental Kuznets curve, which shows a strong correlation between income levels and demand for environmental cleanliness.[79] Most developed countries have gone through similar developments, where rapid industrialization and pollution, followed by higher income and education levels drive environmentally friendly products and practices. While history predicts change, the sheer size and scale of Chinese demand pose a new dimension to sustainability: Are there enough resources on this planet to satisfy Chinese demand? Can China's push into natural resource extraction be repaired and replenished, and can the ecosystems sustain the extraction rate for the time it will take to educate and improve Chinese living standards?

Sustainability and geopolitical stress is probably nowhere as visible as in the Chinese automotive sector because of its relationship to oil. A successful uptake of electric vehicles (EV) would substantially reduce China's foreign oil dependence. With more than 50% of China's oil being imported[80], and more than 50% of Chinese oil consumption coming from the transportation industry, replacing oil with electricity is a political "no brainer".[81] If you project per capita growth of vehicle ownership in China to approach western standards, China will be hopelessly dependent on foreign countries for oil. This is not acceptable to Beijing, and in combination with recent air pollution spikes, maybe the time has come for electric vehicles in China?

In a country of 1.3 billion people, it is more than disappointing that there are only about 10,000 electric vehicles as of early 2013, with 2,000 cars in Shanghai alone.[82] The Government's own goal of targeting 5 million electric vehicles by 2020 is ambitious, but unrealistic if the same government does not set clarifying standards.[83] Simply put, the market does not know if the standard will be either the "charging model" or "battery swapping" model. The national oil companies are seen to be backing the swapping model where consumers can drop in at their existing gas station for a quick change of battery, similar to fueling up the gasoline tank. On the other hand, one has the state-owned electric grid companies arguing for the charging model, where consumers will plug into the grid, effectively buying electricity from the network through simply charging their batteries. So far, the Central Government is holding back on making decisions on which model should prevail and this is severely holding the market development back.

As a consequence, the only sector where development has been relatively rapid is with electric buses and taxis where vehicles come back to a depot at night, or even in between tours, to be re-charged in a regular manner. A version of this was developed in the southern city of Shenzhen where a fast, high load charging system has been deployed, allowing taxis to recharge in 10-30 minutes.[84] This station has now been replicated in 27 cities all over China, and more are to come.[85] Personal cars do not normally have such facilities available, and EV drivers are dependent on finding a charging station close to their office or their destination. For retail consumers, the swapping model may allow you to essentially drive in to a "gas station" and swap to a new battery. This system would however require a standard battery for the different cars, and that swapping stations were cooperating. Unless the Government pushes a standard through, we are quite a long way from such a regime.

In 2009, the Government launched its "Ten Cities, Thousand Vehicles Program".[86] The program has now been expanded to 25 cities, but as long as the infrastructure lacks behind, adoption rates will keep lagging behind. Somewhat optimistically, Chinese policy makers expect local consumers to embrace EVs, because they are not accustomed to the combustion engine the way that many developed country's consumers are, provided they find value in the car. Currently, the high upfront cost for EVs is a deterrent, even though the lifetime cost is lower. A key cost component of an electric vehicle is the battery. An electric car can easily be twice as expensive as a combustion engine car, but the upfront extra cost is offset by three-to-four times lower operating cost, as electricity is proportionally that much cheaper than oil per kilometer.[87] High battery costs also contribute to a slower market adoption, with prices in 2013 around RMB 4,000 (USD 667) to RMB 5,000 per kilowatt-hour. Battery cost per kilowatt-hour is expected to come down to no more than RMB 1,000 (USD 166) to RMB 2,000 in the next five years. A battery package will today cost around RMB 90,000 (USD 15,000) per car, but is expected to drop to about RMB 20,000 to 30,000 in a few years while life span may also be increased to four or five years, or more than a 200,000 kilometer range.[88]

EV buyers in large cities, such as Shenzhen, have been provided government sponsored subsidies of up to RMB 120,000 (approximately USD 19,000) per vehicle for battery-powered electric passenger cars, but demand has not yet responded.[89] From 2010, buyers of electric vehicles in Beijing would all receive a USD 9,600 subsidy per car. For electric bikes and scooters, a trading scheme has allowed for older electric bikes to be traded in for newer electric bikes with batteries containing less lead.[90] Again, lacking clarity on charging infrastructure standards is a major impediment for growth.

China is already in an advanced position in lithium ion battery development and automotive components. Most lithium batteries are made here, and China has a dominating base in rare minerals and components, which are vital for batteries.[91] In 2010, I invested about USD 19 million in a private Chinese lithium battery materials and battery manufacturing company. That is, they produce both the lithium materials needed for batteries and they manufacture lithium ion batteries. While the company has managed to keep itself cash flow positive, which is no small accomplishment given the spectacular failures we have seen for US battery companies like ENER1 and A123 Systems; the expected growth has not been nearly as high as I was hoping; mainly because of lacking market standards. Assuming that the Central Government can collaborate with the industry's stakeholders in developing and implementing a technology standard and growth strategy for the sector, batteries should be a major investment opportunity going forward. In combination with significantly lowering the battery cost, China should lead a revolution in the use of new lightweight materials like graphene and various uses of nanotechnology in the automotive sector to replace the old-fashioned steel structures used in conventional vehicles.

Clean energy subsidies to automakers that manufacture and sell electric vehicles will provide a supply side push for EV development, while ease of registration and use of faster traffic lanes can stimulate demand. Critics argue that while there are lower gas exhaust emissions compared to conventional vehicles, the electricity generated to fuel the cars is from coal-fired power plants that are highly emission intensive.[92] Chinese environmentalists argue that gasoline refining is also a polluting and explosive process. Refinery and rig explosions happen regularly in addition to thousands of daily large and small oil spills from tanks, ships or vehicles that cause environmental damage.[93] As China is a major emitter of carbon dioxide, carbon monoxide and nitrogen oxides, a successful EV implementation would reduce such emissions, especially of monoxides and nitrogen, while also reducing concerns about the geopolitical imbalance of global oil supply.[94] Progress in battery technology signals that there can be a mass application of EVs in urban areas and the Chinese government seem to have decided that EVs must be a key component of China's plan to positively impact climate change, acquire energy self-sufficiency and improve urban air quality. In addition, like other clean technology sectors, it is a sector that China can dominate globally.

Chinese Energy

China has an insatiable appetite for energy with its access and consumption both being highly contentious fields of discourse. China depends on fossil fuels, but is trying to shift towards domestic sources of renewable energy. As China became the world's largest energy user in 2010, the quest for resources is firmly testing China's international relationships and is placing its military in new, distant locations.[1] China asserted water sovereignty 800 miles away from its coast into an area that prompted the Philippines to seek UN arbitration in 2012. Philippine navy vessels charged Chinese "exploration vessels" off the Philippine coast, and Vietnamese survey ships got their cables cut off by Chinese war ships.[2] Military conflicts in South East Asia and territories beyond will surely follow due to China's increased need for energy. China National Offshore Oil Corporation (CNOOC) estimates that the South China Sea region could hold five times more natural gas than China's current known reserves, making it an area that China will not let go of easily.[3]

Access to energy is crucial for China's continued development, making energy efficiency and reducing foreign dependency a prime goal for Beijing. China is now by a great margin the largest coal, steel, iron ore and cement consumer in the world.[4] China also imported over 250 million tons of crude oil in 2012, overtaking the United States' position as the largest oil consumer and importer.[5]   Annual electric power generation growth rose from about 7% in the 1980s to over 12% from 2002-2008. Based on 2010 extraction rates and known economic resources, the amount of resources needed to satisfy China's growing energy requirements is approaching depletion. China's petroleum reserves are expected to run out in seven years, natural gas in 22 years and coal reserves in 72 years, with extraction costs steadily increasing. Overall, the cost and depletion are reasons why coal as a proportion of total energy rose from 69.4% in 1980 to 76.7% in 2008.[6]

China is struggling to strike the right balance to build the energy production capacity it needs, and the sustainable practice it wants. While accounting for more than half of the world's 1,199 new coal-fired power plants under commission[7], China is also planning to add 10 gigawatts of solar power capacity in 2013.[8] That figure is twice the current level, with Government underwriting the sector. Under the so-called *Golden Sun* initiative, Beijing is providing subsidies for rooftop solar projects to incentivize citizens and organizations to purchase smaller solar systems.[9] The boom of the middle class in China is expected to accelerate the need for renewable energy, as electricity demands will increase. For example, in 1990 there was an estimated 200 million houses in China. This figure had since grown to 370 million in 2010.[10]

The shale gas development boom in the USA has caught the world by surprise since 2010, possibly even the Americans themselves. No other country has been as captivated by this development as China, and nowhere is there as concentrated an effort to develop a parallel industry as in China. The Chinese government is focused on exploring its shale gas reservoirs, but it is not clear yet what commercial quantities really exist.

There is an official target of 80 billion cubic meters by 2020, which corresponds to approximately 23% of the total expected demand.[11] There are challenges in both the reservoirs themselves and the markets they are predicted to supply.

First, shale gas reserves in China are thought to be much deeper than in the US, and not as equally concentrated geographically.[12] These reserves are quite similar to the coal seams of China, which are deeply placed and thin-veined. This combination means it is a complex, dangerous and expensive process to extract. Second, there is insufficient water in some of the areas where the gas is thought to be.[13] In the US, even though there is much debate about the polluting effects fracking has on the water used, there seems to be ample water supplies available. Water is becoming a precious "commodity" in as China is likely to further develop shale gas technologies in order to develop domestic shale gas on the scale it needs and wants.

In China, it is the coal companies and national investment firms that are at the forefront of shale gas, not gas producers, such as Sinopec and PetroChina. Few of the Chinese companies with access to these reserves have any substantial experience in drilling and developing horizontal wells below the ground. For example, the companies at present with deals to operate in China include American companies such as Chesapeake Energy, ExxonMobil and Chevron.[14] Chinese firms such as Sinopec and CNOOC are being encouraged to partner with foreign companies, similar to how CNPC created a joint venture with Shell in order to operate in the Sichuan Basin.[15] For a long time to come, China will remain a large importer of international liquidized natural gas.

Consolidation of the mining and energy industry in China will inevitably create Chinese mega companies that will challenge and even overtake mining giants such as Rio Tinto, BHP Billiton and Anglo American. Increased capital access and a large domestic market create unprecedented opportunities for companies such as China Minmetals and Chalco, in overseas purchases and eventual consolidation of thousands of smaller Chinese businesses.[16] As the world's largest consumer of iron ore and coal, China is dependent on developing and processing raw materials abroad. To enable securing foreign assets, China not only needs capital, but potent companies capable of managing international operations.

A number of consolidation deals have been announced to create these new powerhouses. For example, the state-owned mining company Shenhua Coal recently purchased the China State Grid electric-generation unit in a deal valued at USD 8.2 billion. Also, the state-owned investment company CITIC Group agreed to pay AUD 452 million for a 13% stake in Australian aluminum business Alumina. Lastly, Chalco has made several overseas deals worth a total of USD 14 billion in cash considerations over the last years.[17] These transactions are just the beginning of outbound Chinese investments in the energy sector.

Oil

A recurring theme among energy analysts and economists is the correct estimate of Chinese demand, supply and stockpiles of oil. Chinese oil demand is notoriously difficult and critical to judge accurately. Apparent demand is a proxy of total consumption by lumping production and net imports together, but without any adjustment of reported stock changes. In 2013, oil demand was estimated at 9.98 million barrels a day, up from 9.96 million barrels a day in 2012.[18] China is now thought to be the second largest oil consumer globally, accounting for about 10% of global oil consumption.[19]

China is also the single largest driver of oil growth, accounting for more than 40% of global growth alone.[20] There is thought to be significant uncertainty regarding the numbers, because small refiners and operators, referred to as "teapots", in China are apparently not included in national statistics. These "teapots" are important to note because they may account for as much as one-third of domestic production.[21] The Chinese oil inventory is neither well defined nor well known, as numbers are limited to percentage changes, not absolute volumes. Moreover, the classifications are relatively "fluid" with stock changes mostly reporting gasoline, gasoil and jet-kerosene inventories, but not liquefied petroleum gas, naphtha or fuel oil stocks. Based on the numbers it seems unclear whether or not the majority of stocks held by independent refiners are included in the numbers from the National Bureau of Statistics (NBS). The general consensus on growth in Chinese oil demand, however, seems to lie around 4% in upcoming years[22].

The Chinese market for gasoline and diesel is heavily

regulated. Prices are determined largely by the NDRC. In February of 2013, gasoline prices rose to RMB 300 (USD 48) per metric ton, while diesel prices rose to RMB 290 (USD 46) per ton.[23] Price increases at pump stations were at 3.1%, with subsidies put in place to offset the price increase for the farming and public transport industry. Unleaded gas costs about USD 1 per liter as of March 2013 and is generally set by tracking a crude oil basket of oil from Brent, the Middle East and Indonesia, with adjustments being made both up and down frequently.[24] China did overtake the USA as the world's largest importer of oil by the end on 2012, meaning that China's dependence on Middle Eastern peace has never been greater. China not only wants, but also needs stable geo-political development in Iran. That need is good news for global peace.

The need for oil is also good news for the automobile industry. While China has 100 million vehicles today, 400 million passenger vehicles could exist by 2030. Despite that increase, the penetration rate of vehicle owners would still only be approximately 28%.[25] That percentage indicates why it is so important for the Chinese government to strictly follow up on fuel emissions. The penetration rate could easily reach 50% by 2050, and it is a daunting task to cater for the fuel needs of more than 600 million vehicles.[26] The only valid policy response to that demand is to introduce electric vehicles and expand public transportation.

Raising fuel standards could also mitigate this rise in vehicle ownership. The effect of implementing standard V fuel includes an average 78% emissions reduction per vehicle, and at least a 20% increase in fuel efficiency. If the decrease in car usage rates is also added, along with assuming subway system coverage is improved, then the total road emissions in 2030 could be as much as 50% below current emission levels.[27] That decrease would be very noticeable. China had over 100 million vehicles in 2012, with the majority of vehicles only meeting the so-called National Emission Standard III.[28] Shanghai, Guangzhou and Nanjing are already using the upgraded Level IV fuel as of 2013, with only Beijing applying the strictest V standard. In other words, the consumers do not have much of a choice in terms of fuel.

Vehicle emissions are determined by the quality of the fuel. Thus, the higher the quality, the better it is for the environment. The strictest China standard is NES V, which is roughly equal to the European Union's so-called Euro V fuel standard.[29] The standards are distinguished based on sulfur and manganese content emitted upon combustion. In essence, as the standard becomes stricter from NES I to NES V, the sulfur and manganese content in the fuel become lower. Consequently, emissions are reduced for the benefit of the environment. A further challenge in China is that even if new standards were to be implemented; there is not enough standard IV diesel fuel or refining capacity domestically.[30] It must be built, and that again is a Government decision. The National Emission Standard IV has been introduced, but implementation has been subsequently delayed at least twice, because there is no clarity of who will have to pay the bill.

Experts at China's University of Petroleum claim the problem of supplying cleaner fuel lies with the need for a broad upgrade of Chinese refineries' equipment, technology and catalysts, along with vehicles' engines.[31] Meanwhile, China's national planning ministry, the NDRC, stated that "oil companies have had clean fuel overseas for years – there are no technical barriers. It's just a matter of whether or not you want to do it".[32] To progress these matters, the Government should allow refiners to increase prices, which are also kept artificially low and do not create economic incentives. At a bare minimum, prices must be hiked in places like Beijing and Shanghai, while allowing for more time in second- and third-tier cities. In this way, affluent customers can be made to pay part or all of the costs.

The NDRC and the State Council have already introduced the NES IV standards for petrol, and NES IV for diesel will be introduced in 2014. By June 2013, NES V diesel will be put in production, with NES V petrol due by the end of the year.[33] National convergence and requirements for NES V is planned to be implemented by no later than 2017. The State Council has ordered the refineries to upgrade, requesting the Chinese oil giants like PetroChina, Sinopec and CNOOC to take the first steps. The cost addition is estimated to be approximately RMB 300 (USD 50) per ton for sulfur-removal from the fuel.[34] NDRC estimates refiners will have to invest in new equipment for about USD 10 billion to manage these upgrades. China should look at that upgrade as a domestic investment in new jobs, technology and services, which would spread out very positively in the economy. Refineries will have to make the initial investment, but surely the consumers will eventually have to pay the bill, with the exception of Government transfers to the poorest regions of China for a transition period. The cost is, however, negligible for consumers that already can afford car transportation.

While China purchases crude oil at global prices, prices can be altered afterwards. Due to subsidies and low taxes, petrol and diesel can be sold at substantially lower prices set by the Government after refinement. Sinopec accounts for half of

China's oil refining capacity with comparatively lax regulations. As an example, China permits petrol sulfur content at 150 parts per million (ppm) of the oil, while European standards are set at maximum 10 parts per million.[35] The rating agency Moody's estimated in 2012 that upgrading Sinopec's equipment to European standards would cost USD 7-8 billion.[36] This capital expenditure must either be paid for by a share placement or via increased gasoline prices. Shareholders should not protest, Government should insist and management must act.

Coal

China burns almost as much coal as the rest of the world combined. In 2011, China's coal consumption rose sharply by more than 9% or about 325 million tons, reaching a total consumption of 3.8 billion tons.[37] The rest of the world burns 4.3 billion tons and consumption growth is not even as rapid as China's. Chinese coal consumption is expected to peak around 2030, as cleaner energy will begin to replace the installed capacity. As a result, China is investing rigorously to reduce its growing coal addiction.

With more than 70% of China's energy originating from coal, China needs to significantly reduce emissions of harmful particulates, ash and sulfur through retrofitting coal-fired power plants with pollution control technology. Despite the Chinese government estimating over 80% of coal-fired power plants to have been fitted with desulphurization equipment and facilities, the operation rate may be significantly lower.[38] Certain Government figures suggest only 60% of the thermal coal desulphurization equipment is working or "turned on", and even those figures may be "optimistic".[39] In terms of de-nitration technology, Chinese studies indicate less than 20% of power plants have installed such technologies.

Coal constitutes 95% of China's domestic fossil fuel resources.[40] Proven coal reserves amount to 170 billion tons, or 19% of global resources. China consumed nearly 50% of global coal consumption in 2010 and 2011, while accounting for 45% of total global production. As mentioned, of Chinese domestic primary energy consumption, coal supplies nearly 70%. The long-term trend is for China to remain a coal importer in order to satisfy pressures of demand. In 2003,

China exported 94 million metric tons of coal, and imported 11 million tons. In terms of trade, there was equilibrium between imports and exports in 2008. By 2009 China had become a sizable net importer of coal with imports of 126 million tons. Total consumption that year stood at 2,985 million tons. Although the imports constituted a negligible percentage to consumption, they still accounted for approximately 15% of global coal trade.[41]

Due to China's coal imports, certain countries have placed themselves in a strong trade relationship with the country. The largest volume suppliers are Indonesia and Australia, which together accounted for about 50% of total Chinese coal imports during the 11th Five-Year Plan period, or 2006-2010.[42] The majority of Indonesian coal is steam coal used for power generation, while Australian coal is coking coal used primarily for iron and steel production. Canada and the US are now responsible for about 5 million tons of coal export to China, and more than 75% of that is coking coal. Emerging markets such as South Africa, Colombia and Mongolia are also playing a role in supplying China with coal.

The main reason for China's coal imports is due to geography and lack of infrastructure. China's coal resources are largely based in the western and northern inland provinces of Shanxi, Shaanxi and Inner Mongolia. Due to the location of these sources significant transportation bottlenecks exist, which is the main reason China imports coal. More than 70% of proven resources are far from the coal-consuming centers located along the eastern and southern coastlines. The Chinese urban coastal provinces account for more than 40% of total consumption, but have less than 5% of the nation's coal resources.[43] This uneven distribution-consumption pattern requires long-distance west-east and north-south transportation routes that are currently lacking in capacity.

China's current infrastructure cannot manage transporting larger coal volumes. In fact, railway building has lagged significantly behind urbanization on every level, especially in terms of the moving capacity of coal. Capacity in Chinese ports has grown faster than rail capacity, and has proven reliable in accessing coal from abroad. In 1980, railway moved approximately 70% of all coal volume. By 2010, that percentage had fallen below 50%. In the same time period, seaport handling of coal had grown from nearly scratch to now handling nearly 40% of all coal volume.[44] This change has placed the Ministry of Railway as a form of coal and energy regulator and monopoly operator. The corresponding lack of competition has resulted in inadequate rail line investments. The coastal regions have been in competition with each other for investment and import-export business. As a result of this, ports and all related infrastructure have increased steadily every year, causing railway to fall behind significantly every year.

The efficiency of seaports, or rather the inefficiencies of domestic rail, has influenced which regions in China receive what type of coal. Southeastern areas receive domestic coal from the northern ports in the Bohai Bay, and all ports receive seaborne imported coal.[45] Seaborne, imported coal has therefore had an important balancing effect in China, particularly through peak seasons. Many steel companies in China also prefer overseas coking coal for the stability of supply volumes and consistent quality. The environmental consideration is overseas coal has prompted the shutdown of smaller, inefficient coalmines which heavily pollute China. In the same way, new smaller mines have been discouraged from development, thus protecting local environments and re-directing investment to other growth sectors.

On the other hand, this benefit only means environmental burdens are simply moved to other coal-producing nations. In the case of Mongolia, which is a major potential coal supplier to China if internal politics do not interfere, mining operations are largely in the Gobi desert area, and more importantly it is largely open pit mining.[46] Open pit mining allows shoveling coal with giant bulldozers versus the deep underground mining commonly employed in China. Underground mining is dangerous and expensive for many reasons. Firstly, there is risk that water may leak into the mining tunnels, which can trap miners. Secondly, there is also significant risk of gas leakage and explosions. The combination of water filling the tunnels and gas explosions is not only a clear and consistent danger to human life, but it also hosts a number of environmental challenges regarding ground water and soil collapses. The fact that other problems exist in mining goes without saying. With both open and underground mining, risks include acidic mine drainage and toxic coal sludge contamination, in particular with coal washing operations.

Mining operations will always pose hazards to the environment. Any mining operation in sensitive areas can cause the loss and erosion of inhabited areas of wildlife, and thus should not be allowed. Today, coal exports from Mongolia are transported largely by truck, which creates dust and particle problems related to the preparation, transport, storage and end use of the coal.[47] There is also a risk of respiratory problems if coal dust is inhaled, and the only sustainable option is to build railway capacity to transport coal from

Mongolia to China. If railway were built, it would be difficult to justify why the global environment would not benefit from China switching to Mongolian coal.

Uncertainties related to the washing and cleaning of coal remain a severe environmental challenge in the industry. These two processes can be placed in either Mongolia or China, which are both regions with limited water supply. These are arid areas, and coal operations compete with residents and agriculture for water, often resulting in drained groundwater levels. Not only do the governments of Mongolia and Inner Mongolia need to ensure that flora and fauna are supported, especially during droughts, but the coal producing companies themselves are also responsible.[48] Therefore, imports can relieve harm from small and inefficient Chinese mines that are harder to regulate in terms of health, safety and environmental damage. The damage to health is likely to be one of the most shocking statistics. Estimates read that the total number of coal miners killed in mining accidents in China is above 250,000, thus indicating there is approximately one death per million tons of coal produced.[49] As China has become the world's largest carbon emitter, importing coal would reduce China's coal-related carbon footprint, and save lives.

In 2008, I invested in a South African mining safety company called IRCA. It was intended as a great opportunity to bring the company's best-in-class mining health and safety training and certification expertise to China. While the company has continued to service mining clients in Africa, we have not been able to bridge the company to China. This predicament has largely been due to a lack of enforcement of the laws in the Chinese mining industry. People within the industry say most accidents are never reported, let alone acted upon. Local politics overpower central regulations, and it requires a very brave local mayor to shut down a local mine. The closure would send hundreds, if not thousands, of people into unemployment, while cutting the local government's tax income from both the people and mining companies.

Although Chinese mining and environmental laws have some of the strictest codes, it is all for nothing if no enforcement is applied. State-owned enterprises often have lower fatality rates, because they can operate with modern technologies and also access resources, which are larger and easier to mine. China Coal and Shenhua Coal reported that their fatality rates in 2010 were down to 0.03 deaths per million tons of coal. In smaller, local mines run by townships, villages or private local coal miners, safety regulations tend to be ignored and low-quality equipment is used with little or no training. The problem is that throughout the last 10 years, nearly one-third of national coal production has originated from smaller mines with the majority of fatalities coming from those same mines. Estimates show a fatality rate of almost 15 people per million tons of coal excavated in these smaller mines.[50]

There is currently a dispute between the Central Government and local governments over coal mining. The Central Government is clear on its ambition to close smaller mines and grant new generous licenses to larger, typically state-owned operators. Licenses can be revoked and removed, however, without warning causing investors to lose all, or part, of their investments. Some revoked coal licenses are then re-issued to companies where local government profits or personal interests are involved, or more in line with the company.[51] In this respect, coal imports have an important part to play in both addressing issues with the safety of coal mining and corrupt practices.

Starting from 2006, the Chinese government permitted thermal coal to be determined by demand and supply. As a consequence, coal prices skyrocketed and peaked around 2010. At the same time, retail electricity prices have been strictly regulated, with prices set artificially low by the Government. The regulations imply the input or raw materials costs to produce coal have increased rapidly, but market prices for electricity have had an inflation-adjusted real decline. Thus, electricity from coal has become more expensive to produce over the last few years, while electricity prices have experienced a negative real development when adjusted for inflation.[52]

The imbalance between input costs and market prices has placed extreme pressure on coal-fired power stations. These stations are making significant economic losses in many provinces. It is not so strange then that these power companies search to buy the cheapest coal possible, including from the black market. As a consequence, coal-fired power plants often run out of coal, thus leading to "black-outs".[53] Weaker global activities have led to weaker coal prices, and as of 2013, coal imported from Australia[54] and South Africa[55] has become very competitive.

A potential ban of cheap and "dirty" Indonesian coal could have a real ripple effect in 2013.[56] Not only would it provide cleaner coal, but prices could also be sent up. Notwithstanding foreign imports, China is expected to put a cap on coal production, in part to induce other forms of energy. Consensus is that by 2015, an expected 3,800 million tons of coal will be capped, while the predicted coal consumption is estimated at approximately 4,100 million tons.[57] It is not clear yet how this apparent gap will be filled.

For coking coal the picture is quite different. In this case, China's reserves are approximately 13% of global reserves, and more than half of that originates from the western Shanxi province. As discussed previously, it is difficult to access because of lacking infrastructure. Due to the necessity of coking coal in the steel-making process, Chinese steel makers are completely dependent on imported iron ore and coking coal in order to produce the necessary volumes. As of 2004, China has since become a net coking coal importer. Yet, it still produced more than 450 million tons of coking coal in both 2010 and 2011, which accounts for over half of global coking coal production. China imports about 50 million tons of coking coal, which constitutes around 20% of global exports.[58] In other words, China is a large client of the world's leading mining companies. The disparity in China between coking coal reserves and demand, indicates reserves are draining faster than what China is comfortable with. Hence, outbound investment to build up such a supply is seen as a strategic imperative.

Local governments in China seizing land to develop and produce coal or property has caused substantial grievance and mass protests over the last decades. Multiple cases of large demonstrations have been launched against coal mining operators for seizing land throughout the country.[59] Increased imports could imply fewer confrontations in China. Unsurprisingly, it is also the most favored strategy. Countries and continents such as Mongolia, Australia and Africa need to be prepared for China offshoring their social and environmental problems in the coming decades. On the other hand, these countries stand to benefit economically from trading with China. Some "pucks" will certainly be in Mongolia and Australia, if China is earnest about cleaning up its coal industry and intends to maintain 7% GDP growth.

Renewable Energy

The need to develop renewable energy becomes all the more apparent once China's overall energy consumption is further understood. In 2010, the International Energy Agency estimated China's real energy consumption at 3.25 billion tons of coal equivalent. Year 2020 demand forecasts range from 2.34 to 4.9 billion tons of coal equivalent. The aforementioned targets for non-fossil fuels would indicate a forecast of roughly 4 billion tons of coal equivalent. In 2050 however, consumption forecasts rise up to about 6.5 billion tons. This increase corresponds to electricity demand expectations of 8,000 Terawatt hours (TWh) in 2020, rising to at least 10,000 TWh in 2030 and 13,000 TWh in 2050.[60] Increased urbanization will continue pushing that figure upwards for the next 30-40 years.

The Renewable Energy Law formed the world's largest renewable market when launched in 2003, as it laid the foundation for wind-power generation capacity to be increased by 1,400% and photovoltaic solar cells to grow by 3,500 in just a few years. This law has been hailed as the "most successful piece of economic legislation to date" in China. Moreover, China has become the number one green energy products manufacturer in the world, with the potential to remain a global leader for decades to come.[61] The combination of cheap finance and a large, rapidly growing home market is a unique combination never seen before. The Chinese government deserves credit for this legislation and their ambitions alike.

Renewable energy was one of the "Seven Strategic Emerging Industries" mentioned in the 2010 RMB 4 trillion (USD 650 billion) economic stimulus plan. Four and five of the top 10 wind and solar power manufacturers, in terms of their respective capacity and market share, are Chinese. China has overtaken the US as the largest generator of wind power, but the companies and the Chinese government itself are struggling to maintain pace and overview of the market. When speaking with officials in China on the matter of renewable energy growth and regulations, they indicate that changes occur so quickly that it is hard to understand everything. The markets, regulations, prices and players keep changing so fast that the Government is simply struggling to keep up. While the Central Government focuses on national policies, local governments are largely motivated by job creation and local competitiveness.[62] One arm of the Government does not necessarily know what the other is doing. In the Chinese context, it entails that although national policies may be clear, the local interpretation and execution always vary. The winners are often the most aggressive local private-public partnerships where the local businessman gets market share from cheap credit and the mayors get promoted.

Local governments will always have more influence over the practical implementation of policies. Local investment and establishment may be rewarded by free land or low taxes, cheap loans or lax regulations. Often government officials will also be in business themselves, creating bogus business plans to receive government funding and credit.[63] European, American or companies of other nationalities will therefore struggle to compete with serious Chinese players in possession of proper ambitions and easy credit.[64]

The plan for renewable energies under the 12th Five-Year Plan (FYP) is a remarkable document in stimulating use of renewable energy sources and their integration into the conventional energy grid. The FYP calls for renewable sources to account for more than 20% of total electricity generation by 2015. By 2015, another target is for non-fossil fuels to constitute 11.4% of energy consumption, or 478 million tons of standard coal equivalents (TCE). The combined renewable energy production is projected to reach 160 gigawatts (GW), with 61 GW from hydropower, 70 GW from wind, 20 GW from solar and 7.5 GW from biomass. Outpacing projections, industry forecasts show on-grid wind power installed capacity will reach 100 GW in 2015, including 5 GW of offshore wind power, and doubling in total to 200 GW by 2020.[65] A prescriptive document, President Xi Jinping is expected to fine-tune the FYP and push harder in some directions, like natural gas development.

Meeting the 2015 renewable energy targets would significantly reduce emissions of carbon dioxide, nitrogen oxides and other particles. The Government has estimated reductions at 1 billion metric tons of carbon dioxide, 7 million tons of sulfur dioxide, 3 million tons of nitrogen oxides and 4 million tons of small particle reductions. Not insignificantly, 2.5 billion cubic meters of water will also be saved. That being said, on an absolute emissions basis, China's growth steadily creates more emissions. For example, the US cut its total carbon emissions in 2011 by almost 2%, but China "erased" the environmental gains with emissions growing at 9.3% due to increased coal consumption.[66]

As renewable energy develops, certain trends emerge. The majority of the relevant research is focused on energy efficiency and smart grids. Chinese companies will take a global lead in energy saving applications over this period.

Chinese mayors and governors are in intense competition to be the best "new energy cities" or have "green energy counties". These little streams may also support a big river, although that river may be dammed.

Hydropower

Within the advancement of renewable energy, hydropower stands as the largest contributor of sustainable and renewable energy in China. Installed capacity is expected to reach 290 GW in 2015 and 420 GW in 2020, which relates to a growth rate of approximately 7%.[67] The vast majority of this capacity is from conventional hydropower, with the remaining contributions from so-called pumped storage hydropower plants. Among public concern about water pollution, shrinking water supplies and concern about large dams' impact on ecosystems, hydroelectric power remains an area of growth for the Chinese government. Reflected in this focus is the number of large-scale projects under planning and construction. These projects include the expansion of the Three Gorges Dam, the 13 GW Xiluodu Hydropower Station on the Jinsha River, the 6 GW Longtan Dam project on the Hongshui River, and 21 new hydroelectric facilities to be constructed for a total of 36.6 GW of power on the Yalong River.[68] Hydropower capacity growth is likely to slow after 2020 when most river systems are already developed, and the development of new wind power generation is expected to replace hydropower growth.

Ecological concerns related to hydropower are not only restricted to China, but extends to their neighboring countries. For example, it is possible to import cheaper and cleaner hydropower from Siberia. However, local Siberian environmental groups are concerned that the development plans are not up to international standards and are examples of classic environmental irresponsibility. They argue that the local eco-systems will die and China is simply exporting their own environmental problems to Russia; who will have to take the brunt of dam building and the ensuing environmental damage.[69] Similarly, tensions have increased in Myanmar over plans to permit dam construction on the country's Nu River. The Myanmar government recently declared that Chinese-backed hydropower projects are now permitted on the same river further down in Myanmar, known as the Salween River. It seems over six dams are expected to be built along the Salween River, already named the Kunlong, Tasang, Hat Gyi, Nong Pa, Mantawng and Ywathit dams.[70] The plan is to support both domestic electricity needs as well as power exports to China. These dams will most certainly have to be built by Chinese firms, as there is no local expertise in Myanmar for this scale of construction. Similarly, Chinese firms will be involved in building the necessary grids. These dams and the construction itself are sure to send Myanmar's GDP growth firmly upwards.

One can be certain that it will not be smooth sailing though, as Chinese investment in Myanmar has met with problems both in 2011 and 2012, when the Chinese-sponsored Myitsone dam was suspended in the Irrawaddy River further south. China has launched a publicity campaign in Myanmar, which signals a new approach from both the Chinese government and Chinese firms. Having become accustomed to skepticism in Africa and beyond, it seems China is much more sensitive to local concerns than before. China is evolving not in terms of technology, but also in terms of marketing and psychology. In Myanmar, this awareness has resulted in opening plants and construction sites to the media, allowing the media and local representatives to meet with Chinese executives.[71] These measures were unheard of in the past, and illustrate how China has learned from its earlier investments in Africa.

Any way one turns this development, dam construction does

negatively impact the local environment. Only time will show if the electricity will stay in Myanmar, or if most goes to China or Thailand, which cannot be the sole intention as there are daily electricity shortages in Myanmar. On my last visit to Rangon, we had repeated blackouts throughout the day, which was not only annoying but in some cases posed clear safety threats. A 2008 Earth Rights International report claims that a minimum of 69 Chinese companies with multinational operations are now registered and operate in the country, with most projects in hydropower, oil, natural gas and mining.[72]

The immediate problem of dam construction is flooding and that large groups of the local population will be forced to move. Around the Salween River there are more than 10 indigenous groups that will have to relocate, including groups such as the Nu, Lisu, Shan, Karen, Pa-o, Karenni and Mon. On top of damming, the groups are under increased religious and military pressures, with fighting erupting in several local areas. There certainly is a local arms race and a more militarized community as security is increased around dam sites to protect Chinese workers. The locals are arming themselves further, and in 2011, the whole area of the Ywathit dam was "fully militarized" after the deaths of Chinese engineers by local Karenni troops.[73] It seems clear that the Chinese are not the source of the tension, but their presence has revitalized long-standing ethnic conflicts. It seems the only sustainable way to invest and develop the region, is to acquire consent and cooperation from the local ethnic groups as well as the government. This strategy naturally applies to all developers.

Wind Power

Demand for energy in China has also made it the world's largest wind market. Flying over China, you will see futuristic wind mill forests placed all over the country. This scenery is a result of the wind capacity objectives in China, which are the most ambitious in the world. By 2030, approximately 400 GW of grid-connected wind power capacity is expected. The potential lies somewhere between 2 to 3.4 TW, assuming the grid and offshore technologies are adequately developed and upgraded.[74]

By 2020, China targets for a minimum of 30 GW of wind power electricity generation.[75] In 2012 alone, China installed 16 GW of new wind production capacity. China already has the largest installed capacity in the world, with over 60 GW and is prepared to evolve from land-based installations into offshore locations in the next decade. Current installed capacity is only a small fraction of the total wind power potential in China with capacity forecasted to grow to 200 GW in 2020, 400 GW in 2030 and over 1,000 GW in 2050.[76] Wind power alone is intended to cover at least 17% of China's total electricity demand.[77]

While China has the world's largest wind-power market by installed base, the financial crises and austerity measures hit economies and governments everywhere. As a result, global wind energy investments were down 13% in 2012 to USD 78.3 billion. Wind power investments in China were also down 11% to USD 27.5 billion during the same period. Listed wind power companies led downward trends on stock exchanges worldwide, with Hong Kong-listed "Goldwind", China's largest wind turbine maker, dropping 21% in 12 months.[78]

"Huarui Wind Power", a company founded in 2006 had by 2010 become the second largest wind power manufacturer in China. Its company valuation then was in the "hundreds of billions" of RMB. With slowing wind sector growth, "Huarui" has since revealed excess capacity, surplus inventories, heavy losses and sustained quality problems.[79] Its market capitalization has plummeted. Yet, these are the companies that knock out foreign competition, in part because they have access to cheap financing and part may not pay its operational expenses in time, or sometimes not at all. Thus it is no surprise that all wind related companies market capitalizations have fallen dramatically, since most governments have been cutting back in renewable energy investments since 2009. German, British and Spanish governments have all reduced their solar photovoltaic subsidies and US wind installations have dropped markedly in the period as tax credit incentive schemes have expired or been phased out.[80]

The golden egg in Chinese wind power is thought to exist offshore in areas such as the Taiwan Strait or near the provinces of Fujian, Zhejiang, Guangdong and Guangxi. One challenge is water depth, which heavily influences offshore wind energy developments; with wind turbines at depths below 50 meters require floating foundations. China has estimated a wind energy potential of 500 GW in areas with water depths between 5-50m down the coast.[81] Today, there is relatively mature technology for offshore developments below sea levels of roughly 5 to 25 meters. However, at depths of 25 to 50 meters, the technology is still in development.[82]

Current costs for developing wind power are affected by a vast set of factors, including construction conditions, turbine manufacturing technologies and the management and maintenance of wind farms. Industry estimates have onshore wind power costs around RMB 0.35-0.50 per kilowatt-hour (kWh). The grid feed-in tariff level is set at RMB 0.51-0.61 per kilowatt-hour, causing the cost of wind power generation to be higher than coal-generated power. Then again, further technology developments could significantly reduce that production cost, projected to decrease towards RMB 0.15 per kilowatt-hour by 2020, and to RMB 0.10 per kilowatt-hour in 2030.[83] As a result, these production costs could essentially match those of thermal power, strongly supporting a greater application of wind power in the future.

Investment costs per kilowatt-hour have dropped noticeably in recent years, and now stand at approximately RMB 8,000 per kilowatt. Windmills are composed of several parts, including the wind turbine. The wind turbine itself accounts for roughly half of the costs, and cost reductions in the use of materials, design and other efficiencies are expected to hold much potential. In the next few years, the investment costs are expected to drop towards RMB 7,000 per kilowatt. Estimates place current offshore investment costs at nearly double the land-based costs, with a per kilowatt-hour rate of RMB 14,000-19,000. Cost improvements may arrive as turbine performance increase along with the size of the turbines. As of 2013, turbines generally have a capacity of approximately 3 megawatts. Yet, in roughly 10 years turbine capacity will approach 10 megawatts. By 2020, the wind industry plans to launch 10-megawatt deep-water offshore wind generation installations. The Chinese wind sector will be a significant recipient of further fixed asset investments, creating approximately 720,000 new jobs in related industries.[84]

Issues remain when connecting China's wind parks to the

electricity grids and lack of maintenance is reported to be rife. Most renewable energy projects in China have reported that the connection to the national grid has been problematic, resulting in material electricity loss. Reports say that approximately one-fifth of Chinese wind farms are not connected to the grid and are thus not in effective use.[85] As a result, many wind farms are losing money. The grid companies on their side are not keen on paying the premium, agreed feed-in-tariffs from wind farms. Alas, with Chinese markets not properly functioning, some Chinese companies are starting to search for projects overseas. Such an example is Shenhua Coal, China's largest coal producer, which has stakes in three wind-power projects in Tasmania, Australia. Shenhua has signaled a potential investment of AUD 2 billion in the "TasWind" project, which will be the largest wind power project in the southern hemisphere. Two hundred 3-megawatt turbines are expected to produce hundreds of millions of dollars in revenue annually, with Australia being a preferred destination for Chinese investments generally.[86]

Solar Power

With help from state banks and local government, China has forged ahead to become a global leader in solar capacity. Recent bankruptcies and fallen business models have laid much of the American and European solar industry in ruins. The Beijing government recently re-confirmed plans to increase solar-power installation targets to 35 GW by 2015 from the earlier goal of 21 GW set in 2012.[87] Especially in the southern and western regions, such as Tibet, solar-powered technologies and appliances are adopted from industry to households alike. The pledge from Beijing to significantly increase solar capacity is in stark contrast to the general state of affairs in the global solar industry as the six largest solar panel companies in China posted losses of over USD 2 billion in 2012. Solar panel producers are facing a chronic over-supply of photovoltaic cells, resulting in solar panel prices decreasing by 25% during 2012.[88]

One particularly striking, and complicated, example is the solar panel producer Suntech. Suntech was listed in 2006 and began a massive expansionary program. Suntech was the world's top panel-maker in 2010 and 2011, but as the solar power market slowed down in 2011, the company incurred huge losses, large layoffs and was declared bankrupt in 2013.[89] As a result of general overcapacity, several companies have throughout 2013 signaled that they cannot handle debt interests and principle payments. For example, the company LDK Solar had more than USD 375 million in outstanding bonds as of the end of 2012.[90] Although more companies may go bankrupt, they will not necessarily go out of business, because China has too much at stake. In the case of Suntech, the consequences of the bankruptcy severely would impact the local town of Wuxi where Suntech is based. The potential restructuring of the USD 2 billion of debt would become a priority for the local government in order to save the 10,000 employees in Wuxi.[91] Fortunately for Suntech, the insolvency has resulted in a near state-owned takeover for the company, thus the employees are kept and panels continue to be constructed and distributed, consequently exacerbating the glut.

Panel over-supply is not the only danger, which the solar power industry faces. The unprecedented bankruptcy of Suntech is also a function of another chronic China problem: accounts receivable or bad customer credit. The Suntech bankruptcy was mainly linked to customers who bought products on credit, but never paid. The outstanding credit was perhaps never expected to be paid, with the "sales" being booked as revenue, intending to mislead the markets. It seems from information emerging now that around 30% of Suntech's uncollected bills originated from a handful of customers financially supported by a Suntech-funded investment firm.[92] According to Suntech filings, these companies bought products on credit without the intention of paying. Suntech consequently became exposed to a USD 720 million case of fraud.[93] I have seen this scenario occur time and time again in all emerging markets, not only in China. It cannot be stressed enough how important it is for the executive management, board and shareholders of Chinese companies to constantly monitor the relationship between sales and uncollected bills. In 2013, it was reported that LDK Solar had an approximate USD 4 billion debt crisis on its hands, a scandal that could set their sponsor's economy, Xinyu City, back for more than a decade. China Development Bank said relating to LDK that "local government's funds are being used to help firms cling on which should have gone bust, resulting in losses for the green energy sector nationwide".[94] My excellent former boss at Elkem, now with REC Energy, Ole Enger, could probably not agree more, operating as they are in a market with massive Chinese overcapacity and rather inefficient markets.

With global solar demand expected to increase more than 15% in 2013, we may see state-owned banks and state creditors issue new working capital debt to the industry. China has responded to the industry's challenges by increasing the solar power subsidy. The subsidy is a price which solar-powered plants can sell power to the electricity grid, which in most areas as of the beginning of 2013 was still set at RMB 1.09 per kilowatt-hour.[95] This value is triple the price received by power plants, which are currently burning coal for electricity.[96] Electricity grid companies are obliged to purchase power from the solar parks, underwriting their possibly flawed business plans.

Prior to the European Union imposing duties on Chinese solar panels in June 2013, solar panel makers in both the US and the EU launched numerous anti-subsidy and anti-dumping complaints, and called for separate investigations on Chinese solar companies. The original complaint from Europe was from the European solar glass producer "ProSun Glass". The complaint from the industry group was on behalf of solar glass producers, which accounted for over 25% of the EU's solar glass output.[97] The major argument is that Chinese companies enjoy an unfair state advantage, thus deploying unfair pricing practices that can lead to European companies going out of business. Reports have the EU solar-glass market valued below EUR 200 million, while the Chinese solar panel import market is estimated at a value of EUR 21 billion in 2011.[98] Under-cutting the European market by dumping cheaper

Chinese products is a serious threat to the EU solar industry. In retaliation, China is investigating European poly-silicon makers for dumping practices as well.[99] Governments on all sides are intervening to protect their homegrown industries. Hopefully consumers and the environment will win through opposing governments sitting down and negotiating a solution.

For solar projects, the technology and development costs have been comparatively high, yet panels are unreliable and there have been quality problems with Chinese products. Even today, China is importing much of the machinery and materials needed for thin-film photovoltaic cells, because China does not have the most advanced technology available. Foreign investment in Chinese solar power generation is generally not encouraged, because companies with less than 51% Chinese ownership are prohibited from benefiting from the Clean Development Mechanism (CDM), which also includes investing in wind power.[100] Only companies wholly owned or controlled by Chinese parties may carry out CDM projects in the PRC. The Chinese government believes in size and scale. Increased merger and acquisition activity will encourage efficiencies and consolidation may be a way to deal with excess capacity and current market pressures.

Bio-gas and Biofuels

A recent target the NDRC set is that China needs to acquire about 11 million tons of ethanol and 2 million tons of biodiesel to meet the State Council's 15% non-fossil fuel energy goal. Some Chinese agriculture experts worry that this goal has the potential to impact agricultural development and grain security, thus entailing a general worry about food security in the country. A further reduction of agriculture land to grow biofuel feedstock is fueling concerns about food prices and potential ecological damage. The early investment phase of biofuels from 2002 onwards has seen very mixed results.[101] Along with rising food prices, the economics and strategies of biofuels are questioned.

In China, biofuel development has been led by PetroChina, Sinopec and several large agriculture businesses. Quite a few smaller private companies have also entered the industry, which has left the market fragmented and based on multiple technologies. The Chinese government's focus has been on non-grain starch and sugar crop fuel options. The dominant biofuel production feedstock is corn and wheat, currently comprising over 80% of Chinese biofuel feedstock.[102] However, further projects based on this feedstock are not permitted. Thus alternative crops, such as cassava, sorghum and sweet potato are developed.

Due to the farming land shortage in China, additional land for biofuel development is very limited. Current available land for biofuel feedstock in China is at about 24 million hectares, with a corresponding ethanol production potential between 70-80 million tons. Despite these prospects, the targets may be significantly impacted by insufficient water resources, pesticides, fertilizers and farmers to produce the feedstock in tandem with food products. Besides land restrictions, the cost of biofuel is dominated by feedstock prices. Feedstock accounts for more than 50% of production costs. Feedstock that follow market prices are very sensitive to supply and demand. For example, China is heavily reliant on imports of cassava and sweet sorghum.[103] The more China can import, the less feedstock appear to be produced at home. Thus, local farmers shift to higher margin products or jobs. More imports therefore increases China's reliance on overseas products and exacerbates the structural dependence in the economy. There is a vibrant debate in China surrounding biofuels and the sustainability of feedstock. There is also much to support the skepticism towards biofuels with serious questions regarding the life cycle of sugar- and starch-derived fuels.

Moving towards biodiesels, waste food oil is another potential feedstock. In 2010, food oil consumption stood at 26.8 million tons, with 20-30% of waste oil potentially generated annually from that figure. If even half of that waste oil is collected and reasonably recycled, 2.68 – 4.02 million tons of biodiesel could be produced each year.[104] China has had a series of media reports concerning waste oil that had been collected, then illegally refined and sold as low end cooking oil.[105] Waste oil is also used in a multitude of other disciplines, such as leather and rolling industries. Due to its many uses, waste oil is also a market driven price mechanism. The major challenge in China is the highly fragmented collection system, where different recycling plants fight over waste oil supply.[106] Securing long term stable supply of feedstock seems very difficult.

Over the last decade, I have been involved in biofuel

investments in both India and Australia. The most promising projects are the tree- or shrub-based fuel stocks. Many species have been involved, from the largely unsuccessful Jatropha shrub to the Pongamia and Neem trees.[107] China has the capacity to bear 36 million hectares of oil-bearing trees, but the gestation period is often more than three of four years and is severely capital intense. Although a Jatropha planting base of more than 0.2 million hectares has been built, only 40 tons of Jatropha-derived oil has been produced.[108] This output is shockingly low and has nearly killed the tree-based industry. Therefore, another form of biofuel needs to be focused on until a tree-based feedstock like Pongamia becomes a viable option.

There is a drive for a "second-generation" biofuels from cellulosic biomass, where the resource and feedstock potential is expected to be much higher. However, similar to other fuel stocks, the economics to support this innovation do not stack up as of yet. Production costs for cellulosic biomass range from USD 0.6 to 1.30 per liter, which is higher than gasoline.[109] It will be some time before biofuels can realistically challenge fossil fuels from an economic efficiency standpoint. In an environment where governments and consumers are struggling with an economic downturn, there is also less capacity and willingness to sponsor and support higher fuel costs, such as biofuel.

It is reasonable to expect China to continue developing its embryonic biofuel sector, with annual production estimates for fuel ethanol already around 2 million tons of oil equivalents.[110] This estimate could more than double, if the Chinese government introduces policies such as deregulating the industry, publishing sustainable guidelines, increasing the speed of technological developments or introducing attractive economic incentives. If the environment is not forthcoming, biofuels will remain a very small portion of China's energy mix.

Biogas is thought to have more promising potential in China, especially in terms of reducing methane gas emissions. Biogas is created when animal and human excrement is changed into a natural gas. A few studies in China now conclude biogas can materially reduce wood and crop residue for fuel, while maintaining sources for natural fertilization. Natural biogas primarily aims to replace fuels such as wood and coal, thereby reducing costs and indoor pollution for households. If implemented correctly, there are also obvious time and emission benefits from converting to biogas, compared to the time-intensive wood-fired stoves, which require hours of wood collecting. The residue remaining from the production of biogas can also be used as a fertilizer, which is already an important use of animal dung.

Due to lack of technologies and collection infrastructure, there has been a slow adoption of biogas. This renewable energy source has only about 19% of its potential used today. Historically, we have seen several phases of biogas, beginning in the 1980's up until today. Much of the previous technologies have been deemed inefficient and uneconomical. The 11th Five-Year Plan re-introduced biogas as a national energy resource in China, and several projects were subsequently launched. Together with the World Bank, China launched a USD 440 million project in the southeastern provinces of Anhui, Sichuan, Guangxi, Hunan and Hubei. New technologies were introduced so waste from kitchens and toilets could be collected into central digesters. Biogas equipment was provided to nearly 500,000 rural households in the aforementioned regions.[111] In addition, cement containers were constructed and placed near animal farms. Projects are divided between small-scale biogas projects for farms with penned livestock, not free grazing, and larger scale projects with central collection systems. Unsurprisingly, the smaller projects struggled with both the technology and implementation, even though these households stand to potentially benefit the most.

As the farming industry consolidates, this situation may change. By 2015, the estimates are that more than 75% of Chinese pigs will be in commercial farms, which would enhance the biogas projects potential to collect waste for biogas generation. In areas where the World Bank project has been introduced, both higher and lower income households had more than 50% of their energy needs satisfied from coal or firewood.[112] Thus, fuel use in China consequently appears to be more dependent on region, local temperature and the available infrastructure, rather than income. The same study indicated each biogas user was able to substantially reduce consumption of non-sustainable fuel sources. Users employed nearly 200kg less coal, 157kg less firewood and 350kg less crop residue annually compared to non-biogas users. It is unclear from the study if these users would not have used less solid fuels to begin with, because more educated and wealthier households tend to consume less fossil fuel in general. However, the study does suggest some environmental relief. The time saved from collecting solid fuels was used for leisure or generating other income. Adoption of biogas also improved indoor climate and fertilization usage. After subsidies, it costs approximately RMB 2,000 (approximately USD 320) to install a biogas solution in a household, including all materials and installation.[113]

One challenge is that biogas availability naturally depends on the availability of dung. Many users feel biogas is insufficient for their needs, while others lack the technical knowledge or support for the equipment. Other research in China indicates only half of the biogas solutions were in use a few years after installation. Data along these lines will likely deter mass adoption. The solution could be as simple as providing proper training and service for the users. Only 60% of rural biogas users received technical training on how to use the biogas residues, and repair delays were cited as a main factor in use slowdown.[114] These suspensions indicate the need to target only households with sufficient livestock and labor supplies, and provide adequate training and maintenance to release the full potential of biogas as a renewable energy source.

Natural Gas

Another form of gas China can use is simply natural gas. In the 12th Five-Year Plan for Natural Gas Development, China aims for an annual gas consumption of 230 billion cubic meters.[115] Natural gas has the potential to account for 12% of China's energy consumption in 2020 and 18% in 2030. The NDRC estimates China's oil and gas reserves are around 22 trillion cubic meters, with coal bed methane gas production targets of 6.5 billion cubic meters by 2015, in addition to shale gas production picking up to 1.6 billion cubic meters in the same period. The NDRC aims by 2015, 18% of China's urban population to be able to access natural gas as a substitute for oil and coal.[116]

The natural gas revolution in the US could also impact coal markets in China. As the US will consume less coal by switching to natural gas, American coal will become available to China. The Pacific Northwest of the US has built coal terminals that can handle significant volume to China. With growing domestic Chinese concern over unsafe mining conditions, some of that coal could now rather be mined in the US. The coal market is sensitive to supply and demand, and more coal coming online from the US could lead to downward pressure on coal prices in China, making a switch to US coal more likely. There is a battle between cheaper coal prices and renewable energy sources to be played out. So far it seems that coal is in a pretty strong position. A 10% price drop in costs would result in a 12% increase in the volume of coal used.[117] Cheaper coal could therefore act as a discouragement of renewable energies. These intertwined relationships between energy sources are one major complication when investing in energy in China.

The shale oil and gas revolution is irrevocably changing the outlook for the US, and potentially the global energy market. Both early resource estimates and production numbers seem to consistently underestimate actual resources and delivered production. It is bigger, it is earlier and it is cheaper. The North Dakota fields Bakken and Three Forks have just been reported at 745,000 barrels per day, up 2.4% from April this year, and bringing year-on-year growth up 30%.[118] Looking at earlier analyst estimates, the most optimistic estimates a year ago was 750,000 barrels a day, indicating that the industry is severely underestimating production potential and output. The then "wildly optimistic" estimates for 2016 of 1 million barrels a day have now become a much more conservative estimate.[119] In addition, fields like Eagle Ford and Permian Basin will enter similar production levels by 2016.[120] It seems the industry, as a whole, is not really considering the production levels from unconventional sources in the US.

A key driver for unconventional oil production is the current high oil price, but possibly as important, is the short time to profitable production and drilling intensity. Time from drill permit to production is estimated to 4 months, with 40% oil extraction in 12 months, and the remaining 60% in 24 months. The cash flow is fundamentally different than that of offshore development and drilling operations, where one tends to be in negative cash flow for up to 3-5 years. US shale oil drilling permits in Eagle Ford skyrocketed from 26 to more than 4,000 by 2012.[121] Thus, US shale oil producers are at unusually high production intensities now, and are likely to surprise on the upside in the second half of 2013. Positioning your portfolio for US shale oil and gas exposure seems reasonable.

The US shale gas revolution is not lost on China. China is more foreign oil dependent than any other economy of its scale and growth. More than 50% of China's consumed oil is imported, and most of that is spent in the domestic transportation sector alone. With China already having the world's largest and fastest growing automotive market, it follows that China has a lot to gain in developing a domestic shale oil and gas boom of its own. No one knows how much shale gas China has, but the US Energy Information Agency estimates that it is roughly 1,275 trillion cubic feet, which is likely to be a far too conservative amount.[122] Nevertheless, current estimates are already larger than the US reserves. The global oil and gas industry is therefore rushing to China for a piece of the Chinese shale gas revolution. As China's energy demand is set to double over the next 20 years, shale gas could play a key role.[123] Nuclear and renewable energy capacity coming online is not enough to cope with demand, and China is eager to come off heavily polluting coal that today accounts for approximately 70% of electricity generation.[124] The sooner China can switch to shale gas, which only produces half the carbon dioxide of coal, the better off both local air quality and the global climate will be.

China's National Energy Administration has decided to aim to produce at least 230 billion cubic feet of shale gas annually by 2015.[125] By 2020, the objective is raised to 2.2 trillion cubic feet, or about one-fourth of the volume currently produced in the US.[126] China is playing a game of "catch up", and critics argue a lot can go wrong. The process of extracting shale gas, called "fracking", can pollute an already strained water table as well as release large amounts of methane gas, a harmful greenhouse gas, into the atmosphere. Reaching the 2020 targets depends on geology, technology and policies. Currently we do not know if it will all come together. To illustrate how far behind China is in fracking to the US, China has drilled about 60 fracking wells in total as of the end of 2012[127], while the US currently drills about 35,000 annually[128]. That difference is literally an ocean apart.

Shale gas in China is thought to be in three main geographical areas: the Tarim, the Ordos and the Sichuan basins.[129] These areas were thought to be the bottom of lakes millions of years ago, and plants and animals buried there have today turned into oil and gas. As the oil and gas floats up to the top, some of the gas gets stuck in rocks, not forming traditional wells, which have been easy to drill and extract from in the past. Shale is a fine-grained sedimentary rock composed of mud that is a mix of clay minerals and fragments of other minerals, especially quartz and calcite. The ratio of clay to other minerals is variable, but shale is characterized by parallel breaks less than one centimeter in thickness, called fissility. Gas and oil are stuck in "unconventional", non-permeable rock layers and need to be broken up to release the hydrocarbons. To release the carbons, the rock needs to be "fractured", hence the term "fracking". A combination of water and chemicals are injected at high pressure to fracture the rocks and create a way out for the gas. This old technology in combination with new technological developments in horizontal drilling, have made shale gas economical. However, given large water requirements, only the Ordos and Sichuan basins have near term potential, while the northwest basin of Tarim, which is in a dry desert, is less interesting for the time being.

China is short on both management and the latest technology to run shale gas operations, but long on capital and equipment, as the Chinese government is prioritizing the sector. The state owned oil companies are therefore actively acquiring international gas companies. Sinopec announced a USD 1 billion deal to buy a stake in Chesapeake Energy's Oklahoma field.[130] PetroChina, the Chinese oil giant with more than 1.7 million employees, announced a USD 15.1 billion deal to acquire Canadian oil and gas company, Nexen.[131] Surely, there will be more mergers and acquisitions from Chinese companies in this sector. Meanwhile, Shell is joint venturing with PetroChina, in joint statements, their management concludes that the Chinese geology is more complex compared to North America. From the complexity, and the early days of shale gas development in China, it is apparent that the Chinese companies are primarily focused on technology transfer from the West in this phase, yet serious to invest real capital in the sector.

An often-overlooked development bottleneck for shale gas in China is an embryonic and monopolized pipe distribution network. While pipelines are being developed rapidly, and China is the only country in the world that has the capital, the workers and the (lack of) legal system to "just build it" – the real test will be the pricing and operation of the pipe network.[132] It seems to me that the pipelines will be operated by the national gas tanks, and it is not clear if they will have the obligation to take gas into their pipeline, and at what price. If the operator refuses to take delivery from a producer, or to pay market price "on time" for the gas, then private gas suppliers will face a real uphill battle.

While shale development up until today has mainly been a territory for the large state owned oil companies, last year 20 blocks were auctioned to private companies in China.

Astonishingly, these 20 licenses were awarded to 16 private companies with little to no experience in gas exploration and development.[133] The auction winners were either real estate or coal companies all wanting to pile into the shale gas rush. International gas companies could be natural partners, but if the private companies go alone there certainly is an added risk to both development and the environment.

Major concerns relating to the environment with shale gas development include leakage of gas and oil, or other contaminants, into the water table underground. The fracking process produces enormous amounts of wastewater that needs to be treated, and not emptied into the ground, lakes or rivers.[134] The less you know about these risks, the less concerned you will be. The Chinese government has yet to set clear standards on the industry in terms of water recycling and treatment, fortification and maintenance of well casings.

I fear that the Chinese private companies will try to take shortcuts where available, and I urge both the central and local governments to properly regulate and enforce the shale oil and gas industry. Witnessing the revolution in the US, shale gas inevitably has a strong future in China and may develop faster than analysts expect. There is a debate on how involved the Chinese government, or any government for that matter, should be in developing the renewable energy industry. My own investment strategy has been to look for areas where China is "net short". One of those areas is energy sources. This strategy is also not lost on global investors, including those bordering China. Experience indicates the Government should not be too involved in establishing businesses or creating overcapacity. The Government should seek to regulate the framework and provide a stable, predictable and tax efficient system that allows private–public investment to co-exist and prosper. Then, companies themselves will discover the consolidation opportunities and innovation, again given a predictable framework. In most ways, the Chinese government is getting the balance more right than wrong if only looking at China's demand and available resources.

Reforms for a Better Environment

The single most important measure that the Chinese government should take to improve the environment is to continue reforming the energy markets towards market-oriented price mechanisms. As long as prices are artificially low for coal-fired electricity, unsustainable levels of heavy industry will continue to exist and pollute. With coal producers being forced to sell coal to power plants at costs well below market levels, consumers or companies do not bear the real costs of production and pollution.[1] Social and economic goals should not be allowed to artificially keep industries and polluting activities alive. If prices were allowed to be set by market prices, much of the polluting industry and practices would perhaps be required to shut down or relocate.

Similarly, oil prices are set in China with reference to crude oil and the national oil companies' profit margins. However, it would be much more sensible to allow prices to be regulated on the back of crude oil price, pollution costs and gasoline demand. The Government has gone some distance towards this regulation by allowing for a higher pass through rate, but it is not clear how the Chinese government will react if crude oil trades sharply upwards. Nevertheless, the price of gasoline in China remains too low, although higher than in the US.[2] Recognizing the enormous problems China has with traffic congestion and air quality, increasing gasoline prices should be a very low-hanging fruit for the country. The increased car and gasoline related taxes could then be used to support the Party's policies and initiatives in safety, health and the environment. It is mindboggling that the Government is not more aggressive on the tax side of gasoline, given its foreign dependency and also given how inelastic demand is. A sharp price increase will not reduce demand much, but mainly reduce the inefficient and heavily polluting vehicles and industries. I think the tax rate could easily be doubled or tripled without the economy hitting a curb.

Whereas the Government has come some way with at least linking gasoline prices to crude oil, yet not much has happened in the area of natural gas. Hence, there is an opportunity here as well in allowing the market to set prices, thereby regulating who is operating and who is not. While there are varying policies throughout China, prices are currently mainly set on a production cost basis, with some price adjustments relative to other types of energy in the region. This basis has meant that there are large variations on gas prices from province to province, depending largely on supply.[3] In the cases where there is no local supply, consumers pay a very high imported price, while where there is ample local supply the price may even be below cost. The Chinese government must permit and build national infrastructure that allows for price stability and predictability across most provinces, independent of local production. As gas infrastructure is made available, national prices should be regulated by supply and demand of the network and end consumers.

An urgent need for market reform also exists in the broader electricity market, where generators are required to sell into the network at a Government regulated, artificially low price. While electricity generation and transmission ownership is separated in China, and several small-scale private electricity generators have been allowed into the market, the transmission market is monopolized by the state. Pricing is set regionally, based on how much electricity must be generated to stimulate economic activity and investment growth.[4] Local governments may offer companies lower electricity prices in an effort to attract investments to their location, effectively making energy pricing a regional development tool. Local and state coal enterprises are correspondingly required to sell coal below market prices to power companies, while power companies are trying to move downstream in various energy intense industries to earn a profit. Artificially low energy costs thereby contribute to attract industries to regions with no other comparable or sustainable advantage. It is therefore urgent that the Chinese government allows for energy prices to more accurately reflect direct costs. A Chinese household will pay on average about USD 80 per megawatt-hour, whereas the same price in Germany would be above USD 300 per megawatt-hour, and Denmark "leading" the European pack with a household electricity price of about USD 350 per megawatt-hour.[5] There is absolutely no reason a consumer in Beijing or Shanghai should pay less than a consumer in Copenhagen.

China is experimenting with different types of price mechanisms throughout the country. Particularly high-earning or high-consuming households in the coastal regions should be paying higher prices than their relatively poorer cousins in the western provinces. Higher prices should force more focus towards energy efficiency and conservation, while also allowing for easing pressure on the ever-expanding coal generation capacity. There is little incentive for electricity generators to improve efficiency, because they are artificially kept alive only in order to meet development goals.[6] Market-driven and competitive generators would greatly enhance the efficiency of the industry and make consumers think twice about mindless consumption of cheap coal fired electricity. Allowing a pass through of costs to consumers in oil and coal energy, in addition to higher consumption taxes in affluent regions, should go a long way in ending environmentally-damaging industrial policies.

There are huge efficiency and re-distribution leaps to be made by allowing for a more market driven energy sector, with some adjustments for wealth and development.

Water Reforms

The single most important measure that the Chinese government now can do to alleviate the dire water pollution in China is to increase the water tariffs throughout the country. At the same time, it must continue to improve the basic water infrastructure throughout the nation, including the pipe network and reservoirs. As water consumption per capita is rapidly increasing, the costs of consumption need to follow the rapid growth of both residential and industrial demand.[7] Water is drawn from rivers, lakes and the ground and should be priced according to supply and demand. To allow for a certain minimum consumption, particularly residential, a two-tier pricing mechanism where a lower tariff is paid for a basic consumption; with a much higher tariff used once the basic consumption has been surpassed, has been suggested.[8] This mechanism allows for heavy users to pay more and discriminate between the basic and heavy consumers, or at least to start moderating behavior. Prices should be normalized throughout the country, so that water is not wasted in certain areas, while also allowing for scalable water infrastructure projects earning a decent return on capital. Today, there is little predictability and willingness for enterprises to build such needed infrastructure as local governments will not commit to longer term pricing necessary for capital intense projects.

Water rights in the provinces are largely unregulated and non-transparent, with farmers and industries tapping water without control and if they are paying anything at all, they pay very low international costs. The Government urgently needs to regulate water extraction rights and adjust prices upwards. While there are many cross regional committees for rivers and water reservoirs impacting many communities, they appear to be very inefficient in distributing cross border rights and elevate the pricing to manage extraction. Most policies are set locally, with local authorities obviously providing preferences to local residents, farmers and industry. Until there is a national system with strict national authority, there are few prospects of implementing broader policies. Local needs and politics will always prevail. China's household prices of both electricity and water are among the lowest in the world. For example, while the price of a cubic liter of water in Germany costs in excess of USD 2.5, the same liter costs USD 0.25 in China on average.[9] This divide also means that several water infrastructure investments in China simply do not pay. In simple terms, higher prices or more restrictions on access to water will induce both households and industries to look for efficiencies in usage.

As a universal point, I would argue that the Chinese government must do what it can to protect the poor and tax consumption of the rich and urbanized. Higher water, gasoline and electricity costs should be skewed to high volume consumers, such as people with several cars or apartments. The corresponding impact on the less affluent population will be much less, as well as the tax collected could be redistributed to poorer households and poorer regions. Transfers can be made very effective through development subsidies and minimum allowance paid, as well as in public health security and education. The cost of living and consuming in cities should rise exponentially, allowing for more efficiency in urban areas and higher levels of development in rural China.

Pollution Pricing

Beijing should take aggressive steps towards developing a pricing mechanism for polluters to pay for their operating choices. If a company is faced with an inevitable pollution cost, its shareholders, board and management will surely employ a cost benefit analysis on investing in energy efficient, non-polluting technologies. A pollution price incentivizes ongoing innovation in non-polluting methodologies, which will benefit everybody in the long-term. Levied on top of uniform regulations and transparent restrictions, each company will have to question its location, pollution and practices. While still in its infancy, pollution pricing can take on many forms, including quotas, taxes and various trading schemes. The "right to pollute" must become a restricted commodity. Although under great criticism in many countries, the various schemes for carbon pricing are aimed at limiting emissions and meeting global or national targets. Different countries have had variable success with trading schemes, but the principle is sound if implemented rigorously, and preferably internationally.

If not trading the right to pollute, as a minimum polluters must be made to pay for the pollution through taxes or other levies. It is a relatively straightforward concept to levy fees and taxes on high air, water or soil contaminators.[10] The system meets its limitations or challenges in the monitoring and implementation phase, where historic implementation all over the world remains weak. The pollutant cost has to be high enough for the polluter to change behavior, and historically every government struggles to set the appropriate rate – quite often coming out way too low to make much practical change. In fact, pollution prices, such as the average water pollution price for example, have fallen in both real and nominal terms, indicating the difficulty facing local governments in this situation.[11] A recurring problem seems to be local governments becoming intermediaries in the trading schemes as well as randomly determining the price. In such local schemes, with low liquidity, there will be a fundamental lack of trust, transparency and legal basis from which costs are distributed, or even worse, rights are given. A revitalization of the pollution price and collection system seems long overdue.

China should take further steps to develop the fundamental idea of pollution trading schemes as a way to regulate emissions. Pilot schemes are being run in many provinces, and the expectation is that they will be expanded nationally in the next 5-10 years.[12] Emission volumes will be set according to the Five-Year Plans, distributed on a province-by-province basis, and trading will be allowed within and among the regions.[13] There is however little evidence so far that the schemes will be implemented nationwide, and significant uncertainty remains on whether the schemes will create the long-term incentives needed for corporations to invest in mitigation or relocation strategies. It seems that in order for these schemes to be effective, a clear and stable regulatory framework is pivotal, while allowing for Government intervention to handle dysfunctions, especially regarding pricing.

City Policies

As traffic congestion has steadily become increasingly worse, I opted towards driving into the office earlier and earlier in the day. When I had to leave before 6 a.m. in the morning to have a measurable time advantage, and no real difference in commuting back in the afternoons, I have decadently submitted to hiring a local driver. In the absence of public transportation alternatives, at least I can now spend an hour in the back seat each way working, as opposed to drumming anxiously on the steering wheel. Few consumers are in my extremely lucky circumstance to be able to afford a driver, so people are destined for unproductive, immensely polluting congestion. Increasingly, Chinese cities will have to compete for talent and families through their ability to offer reasonable and affordable green communities. Skilled and talented labor will simply not accept queuing for hours or to have their families live in heavily polluted environments. As the economy moves towards a higher level of service intensity, labor will become more mobile. It will be necessary for cities to be green to attract this increasingly mobile skilled labor force.

Urban design and policies will play a huge difference in how successful different Chinese cities will be, creating positive competition with each other. Their ability to build and maintain high levels of mass transportation services will be critical in time management, as well as maintaining acceptable air quality. Offering basic infrastructure such as central heating, clean water and energy efficient services will be absolutely critical. The development of self-sufficient neighborhoods and city planning will become competitive advantages. Compact cities that can address quality of life and environmental sustainability will succeed, while those who cannot meet such challenges will fall behind in both economic activity and growth. The most important take-away seems to be city planners must embrace the development of mass transport and energy efficiency to succeed.

The Chinese government should also further review and improve the systems deployed to limit supply of environmentally polluting activities, such as automobile ownership. The limits currently put on license plates in Shanghai and Beijing are good first steps, but may be improved as loopholes are established.[14] Further moves towards a price discrimination system, such as the aforementioned argument to increase gasoline prices dramatically, will significantly enhance a more sustainable development. Emission standards could be much more stringent and a development towards an electric vehicle-based auto market can be pursued much more aggressively. Critically, setting new standards on fuel refining and the required quality of gasoline and diesel are low hanging fruits that can be improved much faster. Allowing for gasoline and diesel prices to dramatically increase would also let refiners make the required investments faster in cleaner refining technologies.

A stronger framework for energy efficiency in Chinese buildings is also overdue, with energy efficiency per square meter of building floors lagging far behind more developed countries.[15] A framework for design and approval of the use of energy efficient materials is needed, also where monitoring and compliance is enhanced. Going into these new buildings and renovation projects, China needs to step up its energy efficiency labeling system for electric equipment and machinery, for example air-conditioners, washing machines and dishwashers.[16] An audit and certification system is needed and implemented on a nationwide basis.

As mentioned before in this book, it is not primarily in the area of regulation and laws that China needs reform. The greatest need is in enforcement and implementation capacity, governance and compliance. Upgrading SEPA to ministerial status in the form of Ministry of Environmental Protection (MEP) was important, but MEP is not yet really involved in implementation, oversight and control of policy.[17] There is significant weakness in the way that local environmental protection departments in effect are controlled by the local governments whose priorities remain economically driven. The system of national environmental goals meets a significant hindrance in the conflicting objectives experienced by local governments charged with economic growth and new job creation. Without strong central oversight or a fundamental change in rewards and responsibilities, local governments will act slowly on the subject of environmental policy implementation. Low penalties on pollution contribute to a system where polluting is an acceptable cost, instead of actually changing the behavior or operating methods.[18] A significant increase in pollution fees and penalties is urgently needed, as well as holding individuals responsible for non-compliance, both among government officials and industry personnel.

China should increasingly look to shape or adopt best practice policies throughout the economy. Such "best practices" can participate to not only set China on a more sustainable environmental track, but also keep its citizens amenable to the dominant position of the Chinese Communist Party. The

Government must continue to strengthen the monitoring and transparency of the Chinese environment. Efforts to obstruct information or mislead the public will be counterproductive. Official statistics are an important element in maintaining Government credibility, and can be used actively to force polluters and consumers to pay. In addition to making information available, the Government should link targets and responsibilities to the data. One such example is the air quality in Chinese cities where the Chinese government is already committed to such a development. Mayors and governors need to be made accountable for the monitoring, achievement and compliance with national and local standards.

In summary, there is no need for China to sacrifice economic development for a more sustainable future. It can have both. China simply needs to make rapid progress in terms of market reforms and price setting where the affluent regions transfer value to the less wealthy regions, all monitored and managed by a strong Communist Party that holds itself, individuals and companies accountable.

Steady, Clean Reformist River

As China prepares to take over the top spot from the USA as the world's largest economy, it would be wrong to assume growth here is going to be linear or that economic progress will be the answer to all of its problems. Like all countries and systems, it too will surely have its setbacks and crises. The extent that these crises can be dealt with depends as much on the Chinese Communist Party, as it does on its people. The Chinese system will never be like the West, nor should it try to become, given the myriad of constitutional crises and wars that the so-called western powers are responsible for. What the Chinese system will look like is very hard to predict. The Chinese do not really know themselves. It may very well resemble some form of democracy, and will surely be coupled with increasing international power. The military flashes we have seen the last years in the South China Sea are sure to repeat themselves, even on more distant shores with Chinese interests such as Africa or South America. Many have commented that the "hide your strength" strategy of Deng Xiaoping has increasingly been exchanged with a more assertive Chinese diplomacy abroad. The risk of confrontation is not negligible and could be the ultimate price for the "environment". A collision between a US and Chinese fleet in the South China Sea, or a nuclear incident on the Korean Peninsula, are truly scenarios which require the utmost of efforts to mitigate.

It is important to note that the diplomatic assertiveness and China's political line are inextricably linked to its economic development. Chinese economic interests abroad, driven by demand at home, have created a greater Chinese presence internationally than ever before. The Chinese themselves are new to this. China has de facto been an inward-looking power throughout history. Moreover, China has never seen itself as some sort of an international police force, like the US and many European states. China is hesitant that it should part take in such governance with rules largely dominated by American voices.

While some confrontation abroad almost seems inevitable, the greater risk lies at home where any slowdown in economic growth is bound to collide with the changing demographics of the Chinese people. As the labor force is shrinking, China is also rapidly growing older. It is going to take more than setting a limit to how many dishes are allowed at government lunches to reform China. At the core of reform sits the need to free up capital for investments in environmental and sustainable technologies, products and services – many or most of which may directly lie at odds with the economic interests of corrupt officials and management of State Owned Enterprises.

There is much hope in Xi Jinping and the leadership's quiet acceptance of the shift in power from state to individuals that is currently occurring through social media and the Internet. There may be setbacks, but the direction towards a more pluralistic form of government is already on its way. Regular citizens are demanding a transparent and accountable Government. The Party has no choice but to comply and allow the citizens' influence. May these many streams form a clean, strong and steady river.

Appendix

Chinese "Likonomics"

With last year's leadership change in Beijing, the world was introduced to "Likonomics," a catch phrase used to describe the economic policy of Chinese Prime Minister Li Keqiang. With a Ph.D. in Economics from Beijing University, Li is also married to an Economics professor at Capital University of Economics and Business in Beijing, making him stand out from his mainly engineering-trained predecessors. Economists believed until recently that Likonomics meant structural reform, deleveraging and *no* stimulus. We have recently, however, seen other facets of Likonomics that is good news for commodity investors: Likonomics combines reform and risk management with fiscal stimuli and clear growth objectives.

Apparently concerned with a slowing economy, in July 2013, Premier Li launched a "mini-stimulus" underpinning GDP growth. This removes doubt that the new leadership will hesitate to use both fiscal and monetary policies to ensure that growth is upheld, new jobs are created and a hard landing avoided. The mini-stimulus is moderate, directed and paired with wider reforms, where the reforms themselves are also aimed at reinforcing growth.

At the end of June, Li announced new and upgraded plans on how to stimulate less developed areas. Mainly it was seen as a social welfare initiative and interpreted as such. In fact, it is more a combined effort to curb housing prices and stimulate growth as the plans concluded that *"urban development is a key driver of growth"*. Early July, other plans were announced from Li's office involving telecommunication upgrades, environmental technologies and energy conservation. All these measures involve fixed asset investments and Li has commented he wants the private sector to be involved, not only the Government. Later in July, Chinese media reported on a railway construction plan for western China, aimed at developing growth and sustainable development. Thus, the stimulation of growth certainly seems to be a key part of Likonomics.

However, at the same time as he was "stimulating growth", Li engineered a spike in the interbank liquidity rate, sending a signal to banks that their shadow banking operations must change. Banks have to put their wealth products onto their balance sheets so that they can be seen and regulated. Similarly, private lending activities between companies and subsidiaries will also need to be transparent and regulated. Not shying away from painful measures, a more pro-growth reform was the abolishment of the floor on lending interest rates also put in place in July.

As for "deleveraging" the economy, there is little evidence to support this theory. In fact, Li is really behind a drive for "controlled continued leveraging". This also makes sense as the nominal GDP has grown 8% for the first half of 2013, increasing the need for money supply to flow in the system. Both lending and M2 continue to grow in double digits. The liquidity supply is in other words going up relative to GDP growth, but at a slower rate than before. Inflation is stable below 3% and the NPL ratio is still relatively low, largely due to government efforts; providing the policymakers more room to stimulate growth, allowing both monetary supply and lending to increase.

The RMB exchange rate is unlikely to appreciate much further in the short term, as the trade surplus as a percentage of GDP has come down dramatically in the last years. Adjusted for inflation, the Chinese currency has appreciated about 40% since the beginning of 2012 and this cannot continue at the same rate as the average wage increase has been about 20% annually. Chinese exporters are more than "feeling the pinch" and China's productivity gap with developed economies has decreased significantly.

The greater emphasis on environmental change and financial risk management are elements that may cause economic activity to slow, but it does not suggest that Beijing is willing to let the economy go into deflationary territory. More moderate and sustainable growth, yes, but growth for sure. Fiscal measures are more likely than monetary measures, as China simply has too large of a "cash build up" both domestically and abroad. More of this cash will need to be invested and some of it will be spent in November and December 2013 if the administration thinks that is necessary to meet short term GDP targets. The third plenary session in Beijing will see more financial reform and continued directed fiscal measures supporting growth, but sweeping land and SOE reforms will take longer time.

During the 1996-1997 so-called "Asian Financial Crisis", China ran into real difficulties with GDP dropping to 6%, resulting in people losing their jobs and public finances running a deficit. Today, China is in much better shape. There is no unemployment problem, SOE's are (too) profitable, commercial banks are (too) profitable, public finances are in surplus and the government is collecting (too much) taxes. With nearly USD 3.7 trillion in foreign currency reserves, China's Capital Account is in a fundamentally different position than 10-15 years ago. Yes, there has been too much lending and local governments have been too reliant on land sales, but China has never been in a stronger position overall. If anything, central government's debt is too low and debt markets do not function when the size is too small. Part of financial reform in China must include making the government bond market bigger, not smaller.

The risk of the housing markets in the tier one cities collapsing is not zero, but it is very, very slim. Urbanization will continue, and properties in Beijing, Shanghai, Shenzhen and Guangzhou are entirely likely to hold up, if not increase. Second and third tier cities, not so clear, but then again that is where Beijing wants the farmers to find affordable housing. Failed and unprofitable infrastructure projects built in the last years all over China will surely be taken over by the Central Government. Commercial banks with foreign shareholders will not accept this burden, nor will they be asked by Beijing to absorb "ghost cities". Smaller, domestic banks that are exposed might be in trouble, but will eventually be "acquired" by larger state owned banks or state trusts.

Premier Li fundamentally believes in the market economy. Likonomics is pro-growth. Reform does not always have to mean "pain only". Reform can stimulate growth, particularly in private investment. The seemingly unrelated smaller announcements in the summer of 2013 are all related to growth. The reform steps may have little short term impact and we may doubt their effectiveness, but it is evident that Li is driving reform, *and* is willing to use fiscal and monetary stimuli to support the growth of the real economy. Finally, the Chinese government is not monolithic; it is split between "reform minded" Beijing and thousands of "growth driven" local governments. Central and local governments have many opposing priorities and act fundamentally different. Local governments continue to pursue growth above all and still believe it is the best way to promotion. This does not mean the Central Government is powerless, quite the opposite, as they control who is promoted and demoted in the end.

As long as Premier Li wants reform and sustainable growth, he is likely to achieve it. Likonomics may be good for both commodities and the environment alike.

Notes

Preface

[1] Zhang, Dingmin, and Baizhen Chua. "Residents Told to Stay Inside Again, Smog Covers Beijing." *Bloomberg.com*. Bloomberg, 30 Jan. 2013. Web. 19 Aug. 2013.

[2] Ibid.

[3] Chen, Stephen. "Thick Smog Closes Airports and Highways across China." *South China Morning Post*. South China Morning Post, 30 Jan. 2013. Web. 19 Aug. 2013.

[4] Zhang, Dingmin, and Baizhen Chua. "Residents Told to Stay Inside Again, Smog Covers Beijing." *Bloomberg*. Bloomberg, 30 Jan. 2013. Web. 19 Aug. 2013.

[5] Pei, Minxin. "China's Environment: An Economic Death Sentence." *Fortune Management*. CNN, 28 Jan. 2013. Web. 19 Aug. 2013.

[6] Ibid.

Chinese Legacy

[1] Shapiro, Judith. *Mao's War Against Nature*. Cambridge: Cambridge UP, 2001. Print.

[2] Borenstein, Seth. "Greenhouse Gases Make High Temps Hotter in China." *The Big Story*. Associated Press, 12 Apr. 2013. Web. 19 Aug. 2013.

[3] Radford, Tim. "Temperature Rises in China Linked to Greenhouse Gas Emissions." *China Dialogue*. China Dialogue, 15

Apr. 2013. Web. 19 Aug. 2013.

[4] Ibid.

[5] Borenstein, Seth. "Greenhouse Gases Make High Temps Hotter in China." *The Big Story*. Associated Press, 12 Apr. 2013. Web. 19 Aug. 2013.

[6] Radford, Tim. "Temperature Rises in China Linked to Greenhouse Gas Emissions." *China Dialogue*. China Dialogue, 15 Apr. 2013. Web. 19 Aug. 2013.

[7] Hamlin, Kevin. "China Coal-Fired Economy Dying of Thirst as Mines Lack Water." *Bloomberg*. Bloomberg, 24 July 2013. Web. 19 Aug. 2013.

[8] Ibid.

[9] Nathan. "China's Coal-Powered Economy Is Drying The Country Up." *CleanTechnica*. CleanTechnica, 28 July 2013. Web. 19 Aug. 2013.

[10] Sanderson, Henry. "Beijing Air Pollution Tops Hazardous Levels Days Before Congress." *Bloomberg*. Bloomberg, 28 Feb. 2013. Web. 20 Aug. 2013.

[11] Ibid.

[12] Ma, Wayne. "China's Air Pollution Problem: Whose Responsibility?" *China Real Time Report RSS*. Wall Street Journal, 30 Jan. 2013. Web. 20 Aug. 2013.

[13] "China Plans to Invest at Least CNY4Trl by 2020 in Urban Rail Construction." *Caijing*. Caijing, 13 Aug. 2013. Web. 2 Sept. 2013.

[14] Ma, Wayne. "China's Air Pollution Problem: Whose

Responsibility?" *China Real Time Report RSS*. Wall Street Journal, 30 Jan. 2013. Web. 20 Aug. 2013.

[15] Ibid.

[16] Ibid.

[17] Zheng, Lifei. "Beijing Smog Rules Would Shut Factories When Pollution Rises." *Bloomberg*. Bloomberg, 21 Jan. 2013. Web. 20 Aug. 2013.

[18] Economist. "Choked." *Economist*. The Economist Newspaper, 16 Jan. 2013. Web. 21 Aug. 2013.

[19] Loo, Daryl, and Natasha Khan. "Eye-Stinging Beijing Air Risks Lifelong Harm to Babies." *Bloomberg*. Bloomberg, 07 Feb. 2013. Web. 21 Aug. 2013.

[20] "Fine Particle (PM2.5) Designations." *EPA*. Environmental Protection Agency, 17 Apr. 2013. Web. 21 Aug. 2013.

[21] Loo, Daryl, and Natasha Khan. "Eye-Stinging Beijing Air Risks Lifelong Harm to Babies." *Bloomberg*. Bloomberg, 07 Feb. 2013. Web. 21 Aug. 2013.

[22] Loo, Daryl. "Beijing Air Turns Hazardous as Haze Forecast in Eastern China." *Bloomberg*. Bloomberg, 13 Feb. 2013. Web. 21 Aug. 2013.

[23] "Air Quality Standards." *Environment*. European Commission, 03 July 2013. Web. 21 Aug. 2013.

[24] Shuo, Li, and Lauri Myllyvirta. "Beijing Won't Meet WHO Air Pollution Standards until 2030s." *China Dialogue*. China Dialogue, 5 Apr. 2013. Web. 21 Aug. 2013.

[25] Ibid.

[26] Roberts, Dexter. "Why Pollution in Beijing Will Persist." *Businessweek*. Bloomberg, 18 Jan. 2013. Web. 2 Sept. 2013.

[27] Chen, Stephen. "Thick Smog Closes Airports and Highways across China." *South China Morning Post*. South China Morning Post, 30 Jan. 2013. Web. 19 Aug. 2013.

[28] Loo, Daryl. "Beijing Air Turns Hazardous as Haze Forecast in Eastern China." *Bloomberg*. Bloomberg, 13 Feb. 2013. Web. 21 Aug. 2013.

[29] Li, Grace. "Worst Pollution This Year Envelops Hong Kong." *Reuters*. Thomson Reuters, 15 Apr. 2013. Web. 21 Aug. 2013.

[30] Pei, Minxin. "China's Environment: An Economic Death Sentence." *Fortune Management*. CNN, 28 Jan. 2013. Web. 19 Aug. 2013.

[31] Millman, Alexander, Deliang Tang, and Frederica P. Perera. "Air Pollution Threatens the Health of Children in China." *Pediatrics* 122.3 (2008): 620-28. Web. 21 Aug. 2013.

[32] Zhang, Dingmin, and Baizhen Chua. "Residents Told to Stay Inside Again, Smog Covers Beijing." *Bloomberg*. Bloomberg, 30 Jan. 2013. Web. 19 Aug. 2013.

[33] Liu, Linpeng. "Chinese Car and Oil Industries Argue over Air Pollution Costs." *China Dialogue*. China Dialogue, 27 Mar. 2013. Web. 21 Aug. 2013.

[34] Ibid.

[35] "China's Dirty Air Clears a Path for New Investments." Interview by Mariko Sanchanta. *WSJ*. Wall Street Journal, 21 Mar. 2013. Web. 21 Aug. 2013. <http://live.wsj.com/video/chinas-dirty-air-clears-a-path-for-new-investments/066B98AA-8B8D-4DDB-99F3-DB4E4E04ABA1.html#!066B98AA-8B8D-4DDB-99F3-DB4E4E04ABA1>.

[36] Moses, Russell Leigh. "Now Sharper, Xi Jinping's 'China Dream' Marks Departure From Past." *China Real Time Report RSS*. Wall Street Journal, 3 Apr. 2013. Web. 21 Aug. 2013.

[37] Ma, Jun, Audrey Shi, and Michael Tong. *Big Bang Measures to Fight Air Pollution*. Rep. Deutsche Bank, 28 Feb. 2013. Web. 21 Aug. 2013.

[38] Ibid., 19.

[39] Spencer, Jane. "Banned in Beijing: Chinese See Green Over Chopsticks." *WSJ*. Wall Street Journal, 8 Feb. 2008. Web. 21 Aug. 2013.

[40] Ibid.

[41] Ibid.

[42] Lin, Lilian. "Pollution Data a 'State Secret?' State Media Cry Foul." *China Real Time Report RSS*. Wall Street Journal, 27 Feb. 2013. Web. 21 Aug. 2013.

[43] Khan, Natasha. "Glaxo Executives Admit to Bribery, Tax Crimes, China Says." *Bloomberg*. Bloomberg, 11 July 2013. Web. 21 Aug. 2013.

[44] Tang, Didi. "The Big Story." *The Big Story*. Associated Press, 31 Jan. 2013. Web. 21 Aug. 2013.

[45] Branigan, Tania. "Beijing Smog Continues as Chinese State Media Urge More Action." *The Guardian*. The Guardian, 14 Jan. 2013. Web. 21 Aug. 2013.

[46] Ibid.

[47] Lin, Lilian, and Laurie Burkitt. "Extreme Pollution in Beijing Lights Fire Under State Media." *China Real Time Report RSS*. Wall Street Journal, 14 Jan. 2013. Web. 21 Aug. 2013.

[48] Ibid.

[49] Ibid.

[50] Ibid.

[51] Feng, Jie, and Tao Wang. "Officials Struggling to Respond to China's Year of Environment Protests." *China Dialogue*. China Dialogue, 6 Dec. 2012. Web. 21 Aug. 2013.

[52] "Middle-class Blues." *Analects*. The Economist Newpaper, 29 Oct. 2012. Web. 22 Aug. 2013.

[53] "WWF Survey Reveals Major Reasons for Non-green Behaviour among Big City Chinese Netizens New." *WWF China*. World Wildlife Foundation, 29 Aug. 2011. Web. 21 Aug. 2013.

[54] Shapiro, Judith. *Mao's War Against Nature*. Cambridge: Cambridge UP, 2001. Print.

[55] Sinkule, Barbara J., and Leonard Ortolano. *Implementing Environmental Policy in China*. Westport: Praeger, 1995. Print.

[56] Wang, Alex, Jingjing Zhang, Alex Levinson, Kristen McDonald, Jun Xia, Charles McElwee, and Si Meng. *Green Law in China*. Rep. Ed. Isabel Hilton. China Dialogue, Sept. 2011. Web. 22 Aug. 2013.

[57] "Landmark Lawsuit Demands Compensation for Pollution Victims." *Xinhua Net*. Xinhua, 24 May 2012. Web. 21 Aug. 2013.

[58] Qu, Geping, and Jinchang Li. *Population and the Environment in China*. Boulder: Lynne Rienner, 1994. Print.

[59] Zheng, Yisheng, and Yihong Qian. *Grave Concerns: Problems of Sustainable Development in China*. Beijing: n.p., 1998. Print.

[60] "China's First Policy Document." Interview by Chenguang Zheng. *CRIEnglish*. China Radio International, 1 Feb. 2013. Web. 22 Aug. 2013.
<http://english.cri.cn/7146/2013/02/01/3361s746399.htm>.

[61] Ibid.

[62] Liu, Linpeng. "Chinese Car and Oil Industries Argue over Air Pollution Costs." *China Dialogue*. China Dialogue, 27 Mar. 2013. Web. 21 Aug. 2013.

Urbanization

[1] Zhang, Junfeng, Dr., Denise L. Mauzerall, Dr., Tong Zhu, Dr., Song Liang, Dr., Majid Ezzati, Dr., and Justin V. Remais, Dr. *Environmental Health in China: Progress towards Clean Air and Safe Water*. Rep. China Water Risk, 27 Mar. 2010. Web. 22 Aug. 2013.

[2] Woetzel, Jonathan, Lenny Mendonca, Janamitra Devan, Stefano Negri, Yangmei Hu, Luke Jordan, Xiujun Li, Alexander Maasry, Geoff Tsen, and Flora Yu. *Preparing for China's Urban Billion*. Rep. McKinsey & Company, Mar. 2009. Web. 22 Aug. 2013.

[3] Silverstein, Michael J. "Behind China's Roaring Solar Industry." *HBR Blog Network*. Harvard Business Review, 11 Jan. 2013. Web. 22 Aug.

2013.

[4] Ibid.

[5] Woetzel, Jonathan, Lenny Mendonca, Janamitra Devan, Stefano Negri, Yangmei Hu, Luke Jordan, Xiujun Li, Alexander Maasry, Geoff Tsen, and Flora Yu. *Preparing for China's Urban Billion*. Rep. McKinsey & Company, Mar. 2009. Web. 22 Aug. 2013.

[6] Ibid., 18.

[7] OECD (2013), *OECD Economic Surveys: China 2013*, OECD Publishing. *http://dx.doi.org/10.1787/eco_surveys-chn-2013-en*

[8] "China's First Policy Document." Interview by Chenguang Zheng. *CRIEnglish*. China Radio International, 1 Feb. 2013. Web. 22 Aug. 2013.
<http://english.cri.cn/7146/2013/02/01/3361s746399.htm>.

[9] Ruwitch, John, and Hui Li. "China Eyes Residence Permits to Replace Divisive Hukou System." *Reuters*. Thomson Reuters, 06 Mar. 2013. Web. 22 Aug. 2013.

[10] Ibid.

[11] Woetzel, Jonathan, Lenny Mendonca, Janamitra Devan, Stefano Negri, Yangmei Hu, Luke Jordan, Xiujun Li, Alexander Maasry, Geoff Tsen, and Flora Yu. *Preparing for China's Urban Billion*. Rep. McKinsey & Company, Mar. 2009. Web. 22 Aug. 2013.

[12] Ibid., 30.

[13] Ibid., 119.

[14] Ibid., 405.

[15] Ibid., 435.

[16] Ibid., 441.

[17] Ibid., 444.

[18] Ibid., 445.

[19] Wang, Tao. "Why China Doesn't Need More Airports." *China Dialogue*. China Dialogue, 27 Mar. 2013. Web. 22 Aug. 2013.

[20] Hornby, Lucy, and Jane Lee. "China's Urbanization Drive Leaves Migrant Workers out in the Cold." *Reuters*. Thomson Reuters, 30 Jan. 2013. Web. 22 Aug. 2013.

[21] Ibid.

[22] Song, Aly. "Living in a Shipping Container." *Reuters*. Thomson Reuters, 4 Mar. 2013. Web. 22 Aug. 2013.

[23] Hornby, Lucy, and Jane Lee. "China's Urbanization Drive Leaves Migrant Workers out in the Cold." *Reuters*. Thomson Reuters, 30 Jan. 2013. Web. 22 Aug. 2013.

[24] Woetzel, Jonathan, Lenny Mendonca, Janamitra Devan, Stefano Negri, Yangmei Hu, Luke Jordan, Xiujun Li, Alexander Maasry, Geoff Tsen, and Flora Yu. *Preparing for China's Urban Billion*. Rep. McKinsey & Company, Mar. 2009. Web. 22 Aug. 2013.

[25] Culpan, Tim. "Foxconn Inland China Push Spurred by Labor, BI Says." *Bloomberg*. Bloomberg, 4 Mar. 2013. Web. 23 Aug. 2013.

[26] "Population Aged 15-59 (thousands)." *UN Data*. United Nations, 25 Aug. 2011. Web. 23 Aug. 2013.

[27] "Population Aged 65 or over (thousands)." *UN Data*. United Nations, 25 Aug. 2011. Web. 23 Aug. 2013.

[28] Hamlin, Kevin, and Xin Zhou. "Foxconn Plant in Peanut Field Shows Labor Eroding China Edge." *Bloomberg*. Bloomberg, 27 Mar. 2013. Web. 23 Aug. 2013.

[29] Culpan, Tim. "Foxconn Inland China Push Spurred by Labor, BI Says." *Bloomberg*. Bloomberg, 4 Mar. 2013. Web. 23 Aug. 2013.

[30] Hamlin, Kevin, and Xin Zhou. "Foxconn Plant in Peanut Field Shows Labor Eroding China Edge." *Bloomberg*. Bloomberg, 27 Mar. 2013. Web. 23 Aug. 2013.

[31] Ibid.

[32] Silk, Richard. "For Empty Offices in China, It's Location, Location, Location." *China Real Time Report RSS*. Wall Street Journal, 15 Apr. 2013. Web. 23 Aug. 2013.

[33] Lee, Melanie. "Insight: China's 2020 Consumer Is in a Town You've Never Heard of." *Reuters*. Thomson Reuters, 18 Apr. 2013. Web. 23 Aug. 2013.

[34] Ibid.

[35] Ibid.

[36] Ho, Alexandra. "Cadillac Targets Smaller Chinese Cities for Luxury Market Share." *Bloomberg*. Bloomberg, 21 Apr. 2013. Web. 23 Aug. 2013.

[37] Wang, Aileen, and Nick Edwards. "China Issues Plan to Rejuvenate Old Industrial Base." *Reuters*. Thomson Reuters, 2 Apr. 2013. Web. 23 Aug. 2013.

[38] Ibid.

[39] Zhou, Xin. "Beijing, Shanghai Add to Home Curbs as China Acts to Cool Market."*Bloomberg*. Bloomberg, 31 Mar. 2013. Web. 23 Aug. 2013.

[40] Ibid.

[41] Hornby, Lucy, and Jane Lee. "China's Urbanization Drive Leaves Migrant Workers out in the Cold." *Reuters*. Thomson Reuters, 30 Jan. 2013. Web. 22 Aug. 2013.

[42] Cao, Bonnie, and Dingmin Zhang. "China Housing Slaves Helping Property Rebound: Mortgages." *Bloomberg*. Bloomberg, 19 Feb. 2013. Web. 23 Aug. 2013.

[43] Ibid.

[44] Ibid.

[45] Ibid.

[46] Ibid.

[47] Hornby, Lucy, and Jane Lee. "China's Urbanization Drive Leaves Migrant Workers out in the Cold." *Reuters*. Thomson Reuters, 30 Jan. 2013. Web. 22 Aug. 2013.

[48] "Rebalancing the Economy: Bottoms up." *Economist*. The Economist Newspaper, 30 Mar. 2013. Web. 23 Aug. 2013.

[49] Hornby, Lucy, and Jane Lee. "China's Urbanization Drive Leaves Migrant Workers out in the Cold." *Reuters*. Thomson Reuters, 30 Jan. 2013. Web. 22 Aug. 2013.

[50] Browne, Andrew. "Analyst: I Ain't Afraid of No 'Ghost Cities'." *China Real Time Report RSS*. Wall Street Journal, 27 Feb. 2013. Web. 23 Aug. 2013.

[51] Wang, Tao. "Why China Doesn't Need More Airports." *China Dialogue*. China Dialogue, 27 Mar. 2013. Web. 22 Aug. 2013.

[52] Ibid.

[53] Ibid.

[54] Ho, Alexandra. "China Vehicle Population Hits 240 Million as Smog Engulfs Cities." *Bloomberg*. Bloomberg, 31 Jan. 2013. Web. 25 Aug. 2013.

[55] Qi, Liyan. "China's Urbanization Risk: Magnified Unrest." *China Real Time Report RSS*. Wall Street Journal, 8 Feb. 2013. Web. 25 Aug. 2013.

[56] Pomfret, James. "Scuffles Flare at Liberal Chinese Newspaper in Protest over Censorship." *Reuters*. Thomson Reuters, 08 Jan. 2013. Web. 25 Aug. 2013.

[57] Lee, Melanie. "Insight: China's 2020 Consumer Is in a Town You've Never Heard of." *Reuters*. Thomson Reuters, 18 Apr. 2013. Web. 23 Aug. 2013.

[58] Ibid.

[59] Ho, Alexandra. "Cadillac Targets Smaller Chinese Cities for Luxury Market Share." *Bloomberg*. Bloomberg, 21 Apr. 2013. Web. 23 Aug. 2013.

[60] Ibid.

[61] Zheng, Lifei. "China Services Job Gains Key for Shift to

Consumption." *Bloomberg*. Bloomberg, 19 Feb. 2013. Web. 25 Aug. 2013.

[62] Ibid.

[63] Ibid.

[64] "Rebalancing the Economy: Bottoms up." *Economist*. The Economist Newspaper, 30 Mar. 2013. Web. 23 Aug. 2013.

[65] Ibid.

[66] Ibid.

[67] Ibid.

[68] Shen, Feifei. "China Sets Minimum Water-Resource Fees by 2015 to Promote Reform." *Bloomberg*. Bloomberg, 14 Jan. 2013. Web. 25 Aug. 2013.

[69] Spencer, Jane. "China Pays Steep Price As Textile Exports Boom." *WSJ*. Wall Street Journal, 22 Aug. 2007. Web. 26 Aug. 2013.

[70] Ibid.

[71] Ibid.

[72] Zhou, Wanqing. "From Famine to Food Waste: Time to Reflect." *China Dialogue*. China Dialogue, 12 Feb. 2013. Web. 26 Aug. 2013.

[73] Ibid.

[74] Jianqiang, Liu. "China's New "middle Class" Environmental Protests." *China Dialogue*. China Dialogue, 2 Jan. 2013. Web. 21

Aug. 2013.

[75] Masuda, Yoko. "New Japan-China Air Tensions: Smog." *Japan Real Time RSS*. Wall Street Journal, 8 Feb. 2013. Web. 26 Aug. 2013.

[76] Pesek, William. "China's Poison Air Is Becoming Its Leading Export." *Bloomberg*. Bloomberg, 21 Mar. 2013. Web. 26 Aug. 2013.

[77] Shapiro, Judith. *China's Environmental Challenges*. Cambridge: Polity, 2012. Print.

[78] Ibid., 145.

[79] Richmond, Amy. "Environmental Kuznets Curve." *Encyclopedia of Earth*. Encyclopedia of Earth, 4 Dec. 2007. Web. 26 Aug. 2013.

[80] Katakey, Rakteem, Aibing Guo, and Sarah Chen. "China Joining U.S. Shale Renaissance With $40 Billion." *Bloomberg*. Bloomberg, 06 Mar. 2013. Web. 26 Aug. 2013.

[81] Wang, Haibo. *Characteristics and Trends of China's Oil Demand*. Rep. World Energy Council, 2010. Web. 26 Aug. 2013.

[82] "China's Move Toward Electric Cars Stalls." Interview by Deborah Kan. *China Real Time Report RSS*. Wall Street Journal, 20 Mar. 2013. Web. 26 Aug. 2013. <http://blogs.wsj.com/chinarealtime/2013/03/20/chinas-move-toward-electric-cars-stalls/>.

[83] Ibid.

[84] *The China New Energy Vehicles Program: Challenges and Opportunities*. Rep. World Bank, Apr. 2011. Web. 26 Aug. 2013.

[85] Ibid., 15.

[86] Ibid., 1.

[87] Ibid., 3.

[88] Ibid., 13.

[89] Ibid.

[90] Troszkiewicz, Agnieszka. "E-Bike Boom Hits Lead on Chinese Recycled Batteries: Commodities." *Bloomberg*. Bloomberg, 19 Feb. 2013. Web. 26 Aug. 2013.

[91] *The China New Energy Vehicles Program: Challenges and Opportunities*. Rep. World Bank, Apr. 2011. Web. 26 Aug. 2013.

[92] Zhang, Junfeng, Dr., Denise L. Mauzerall, Dr., Tong Zhu, Dr., Song Liang, Dr., Majid Ezzati, Dr., and Justin V. Remais, Dr. *Environmental Health in China: Progress towards Clean Air and Safe Water*. Rep. China Water Risk, 27 Mar. 2010. Web. 22 Aug. 2013.

[93] *The China New Energy Vehicles Program: Challenges and Opportunities*. Rep. World Bank, Apr. 2011. Web. 26 Aug. 2013.

[94] Ibid., 5.

Chinese Energy

[1] Kate, Daniel Ten. "China's Truman-Style Resource Quest Tests UN Law and Neighbors." *Bloomberg*. Bloomberg, 19 Feb. 2013. Web. 26 Aug. 2013.

[2] Ibid.

[3] Ibid.

[4] "China's Energy Consumption per Unit of GDP Drops 4.01% in 2010." *People's Daily Online*. People's Daily, 28 Feb. 2011. Web. 26 Aug. 2013.

[5] Iversen, Morten. "Importing." *Dagens Næringsliv* [Oslo] 6 Mar. 2013: n. pag. Print.

[6] Howell, Thomas R., William A. Noellert, Gregory Hume, and Alan Wm Wolff. *China's Promotion of the Renewable Electric Power Equipment Industry*. Rep. National Foreign Trade Council, 1 Mar. 2010. Web. 27 Aug. 2013.

[7] Zadek, Simon. "China Key in Move to Green Economy, Global Leaders Told at Davos." *China Dialogue*. China Dialogue, 21 Jan. 2013. Web. 27 Aug. 2013.

[8] Silverstein, Michael J. "Behind China's Roaring Solar Industry." *HBR Blog Network*. Harvard Business Review, 11 Jan. 2013. Web. 22 Aug. 2013.

[9] Ibid.

[10] Ibid.

[11] Haas, Benjamin, and Rakteem Katakey. "China's Shale Gas No Revolution as Price Imperils Output: Energy." *Bloomberg*. Bloomberg, 19 Feb. 2013. Web. 27 Aug. 2013.

[12] Chen, Aizhu. "China's Ragtag Shale Army a Long Way from Revolution." *Reuters*. Thomson Reuters, 10 Mar. 2013. Web. 27 Aug. 2013.

[13] Feodoroff, Timothe, and Jennifer Franco. "Chinese Fracking

Plans Prompt "water-grabbing" Fears." *China Dialogue*. China Dialogue, 11 Mar. 2013. Web. 27 Aug. 2013.

[14] Ibid.

[15] Ibid.

[16] Wu, Zijing, and Helen Yuan. "China Seen Creating Its Own BHP to Boost Purchases Abroad." *Bloomberg*. Bloomberg, 05 Mar. 2013. Web. 27 Aug. 2013.

[17] Ibid.

[18] Hall, Simon. "IEA Tweaks How It Arrives at China Oil Demand." *WSJ*. Wall Street Journal, 13 Feb. 2013. Web. 27 Aug. 2013.

[19] Ibid.

[20] Ibid.

[21] Ibid.

[22] Ibid.

[23] Zhou, Xin. "China to Increase Fuel Prices for First Time Since September." *Bloomberg*. Bloomberg, 24 Feb. 2013. Web. 27 Aug. 2013.

[24] Ibid.

[25] Ma, Jun, Audrey Shi, and Michael Tong. *Big Bang Measures to Fight Air Pollution*. Rep. Deutsche Bank, 28 Feb. 2013. Web. 21 Aug. 2013.

[26] Ibid., 31.

[27] Ibid., 32.

[28] Liu, Linpeng. "Chinese Car and Oil Industries Argue over Air Pollution Costs." *China Dialogue*. China Dialogue, 27 Mar. 2013. Web. 21 Aug. 2013.

[29] Ibid.

[30] Ibid.

[31] Ibid.

[32] Ibid.

[33] Ibid.

[34] Ibid.

[35] "Oil in China: Smog and Mirrors." *Economist*. The Economist Newspaper, 16 Feb. 2013. Web. 27 Aug. 2013.

[36] Ibid.

[37] Plumer, Brad. "China Now Burning as Much Coal as the Rest of the World Combined." *Washington Post*. Washington Post, 29 Jan. 2012. Web. 27 Aug. 2013.

[38] Ma, Jun, Audrey Shi, and Michael Tong. *Big Bang Measures to Fight Air Pollution*. Rep. Deutsche Bank, 28 Feb. 2013. Web. 21 Aug. 2013.

[39] Ibid., 29.

[40] Tu, Kevin Jianjun, and Sabine Johnson-Reiser. *Understanding China's Rising Coal Imports*. Rep. Carnegie Endowment for

International Peace, 16 Feb. 2012. Web. 27 Aug. 2013.

[41] Ibid., 3.

[42] Ibid.

[43] Ibid., 5.

[44] Ibid.

[45] Ibid.

[46] Watts, Jonathan. "Gobi Mega-mine Puts Mongolia on Brink of World's Greatest Resource Boom." *The Guardian*. The Guardian, 7 Nov. 2011. Web. 27 Aug. 2013.

[47] Ibid.

[48] Ibid.

[49] Tu, Kevin Jianjun, and Sabine Johnson-Reiser. *Understanding China's Rising Coal Imports*. Rep. Carnegie Endowment for International Peace, 16 Feb. 2012. Web. 27 Aug. 2013.

[50] Ibid., 9.

[51] Ibid.

[52] Ibid., 10.

[53] Ibid.

[54] Kebede, Rebekah. "Asia Coal-Australian Thermal Coal Steady in Sparse Trade." *Reuters*. Thomson Reuters, 26 July 2013. Web. 27 Aug. 2013.

[55] McGarrity, John. "South African Coal Prices Rise on Strike Talk, Higher Demand." *Reuters*. Thomson Reuters, 13 Aug. 2013. Web. 28 Aug. 2013.

[56] Wulandari, Fitri. "China Coal Import Ban Unlikely on Cost, Indonesian Miners Say." *Bloomberg*. Bloomberg, 05 June 2013. Web. 28 Aug. 2013.

[57] Tu, Kevin Jianjun, and Sabine Johnson-Reiser. *Understanding China's Rising Coal Imports*. Rep. Carnegie Endowment for International Peace, 16 Feb. 2012. Web. 27 Aug. 2013.

[58] Ibid., 12.

[59] Ibid.

[60] Wang, Zhongying, Jingli Shi, and Yongqiang Zhao. *Technology Roadmap: China Wind Energy Development Roadmap 2050*. Rep. International Energy Agency, Oct. 2011. Web. 28 Aug. 2013.

[61] Xie, Dan. "Crisis for Local Economies as China's Green Energy Sector Crashes." *China Dialogue*. China Dialogue, 31 Jan. 2013. Web. 28 Aug. 2013.

[62] Ibid.

[63] Chen, Aizhu. "China's Ragtag Shale Army a Long Way from Revolution." *Reuters*. Thomson Reuters, 10 Mar. 2013. Web. 27 Aug. 2013.

[64] "China's Dirty Air Clears a Path for New Investments." Interview by Mariko Sanchanta. *WSJ*. Wall Street Journal, 21 Mar. 2013. Web. 21 Aug. 2013. <http://live.wsj.com/video/chinas-dirty-air-clears-a-path-for-new-investments/066B98AA-8B8D-4DDB-99F3-DB4E4E04ABA1.html#!066B98AA-8B8D-4DDB-99F3-

DB4E4E04ABA1>.

[65] *China 12th Five-Year Plan for Renewable Energy Development (2011-2015)*. Rep. China National Renewable Energy Centre, Sept. 2012. Web. 28 Aug. 2013.

[66] Plumer, Brad. "U.S. Cut Its Carbon Emissions in 2011 — but China Erased the Gains." *Washington Post*. The Washington Post, 25 May 2012. Web. 28 Aug. 2013.

[67] *China 12th Five-Year Plan for Renewable Energy Development (2011-2015)*. Rep. China National Renewable Energy Centre, Sept. 2012. Web. 28 Aug. 2013.

[68] Howell, Thomas R., William A. Noellert, Gregory Hume, and Alan Wm Wolff. *China's Promotion of the Renewable Electric Power Equipment Industry*. Rep. National Foreign Trade Council, 1 Mar. 2010. Web. 27 Aug. 2013.

[69] Johnson, Jenny. "Chinese Investors Targeted in Campaign against Siberian Dams." *China Dialogue*. China Dialogue, 28 Mar. 2013. Web. 28 Aug. 2013.

[70] Mang, Grace, and Katy Yan. "China-backed Dams Escalating Ethnic Tension in Myanmar." *China Dialogue*. China Dialogue, 26 Mar. 2013. Web. 28 Aug. 2013.

[71] Ibid.

[72] Ibid.

[73] Ibid.

[74] Ma, Jun, Audrey Shi, and Michael Tong. *Big Bang Measures to Fight Air Pollution*. Rep. Deutsche Bank, 28 Feb. 2013. Web. 21 Aug. 2013.

[75] Ibid., 28.

[76] "China Was World's Largest Wind Market in 2012." *Bloomberg New Energy Finance*. Bloomberg, 4 Feb. 2013. Web. 28 Aug. 2013.

[77] Wang, Zhongying, Jingli Shi, and Yongqiang Zhao. *Technology Roadmap: China Wind Energy Development Roadmap 2050*. Rep. International Energy Agency, Oct. 2011. Web. 28 Aug. 2013.

[78] Paton, James. "China Tracks Errol Flynn in Quest for New Wind Markets." *Bloomberg*. Bloomberg, 24 Jan. 2013. Web. 28 Aug. 2013.

[79] Xie, Dan. "Crisis for Local Economies as China's Green Energy Sector Crashes." *China Dialogue*. China Dialogue, 31 Jan. 2013. Web. 28 Aug. 2013.

[80] Zadek, Simon. "China Key in Move to Green Economy, Global Leaders Told at Davos." *China Dialogue*. China Dialogue, 21 Jan. 2013. Web. 27 Aug. 2013.

[81] Wang, Zhongying, Jingli Shi, and Yongqiang Zhao. *Technology Roadmap: China Wind Energy Development Roadmap 2050*. Rep. International Energy Agency, Oct. 2011. Web. 28 Aug. 2013.

[82] Ma, Jun, Audrey Shi, and Michael Tong. *Big Bang Measures to Fight Air Pollution*. Rep. Deutsche Bank, 28 Feb. 2013. Web. 21 Aug. 2013.

[83] Wang, Zhongying, Jingli Shi, and Yongqiang Zhao. *Technology Roadmap: China Wind Energy Development Roadmap 2050*. Rep. International Energy Agency, Oct. 2011. Web. 28 Aug. 2013.

[84] Ibid., 7.

[85] "China Was World's Largest Wind Market in 2012." *Bloomberg New Energy Finance*. Bloomberg, 4 Feb. 2013. Web. 28 Aug. 2013.

[86] Paton, James. "China Tracks Errol Flynn in Quest for New Wind Markets." *Bloomberg*. Bloomberg, 24 Jan. 2013. Web. 28 Aug. 2013.

[87] Roca, Marc. "China Drives Record Solar Growth Becoming Biggest Market." *Bloomberg*. Bloomberg, 08 Mar. 2013. Web. 28 Aug. 2013.

[88] Shen, Feifei. "Deadly China Pollution Breathes New Life Into Solar Debt." *Bloomberg*. Bloomberg, 07 Feb. 2013. Web. 28 Aug. 2013.

[89] Goossens, Ehren, and Marc Roca. "Solar Glut Survives Suntech as Customers Seek Alternative." *Bloomberg*. Bloomberg, 22 Mar. 2013. Web. 28 Aug. 2013.

[90] Shen, Feifei. "Deadly China Pollution Breathes New Life Into Solar Debt." *Bloomberg*. Bloomberg, 07 Feb. 2013. Web. 28 Aug. 2013.

[91] Goossens, Ehren, and Marc Roca. "Solar Glut Survives Suntech as Customers Seek Alternative." *Bloomberg*. Bloomberg, 22 Mar. 2013. Web. 28 Aug. 2013.

[92] Sandler, Linda. "Suntech Unit Bankruptcy Had Roots in Deadbeat Customers." *Bloomberg*. Bloomberg, 03 Apr. 2013. Web. 28 Aug. 2013.

[93] Ibid.

[94] Xie, Dan. "Crisis for Local Economies as China's Green Energy

Sector Crashes." *China Dialogue*. China Dialogue, 31 Jan. 2013. Web. 28 Aug. 2013.

[95] Shen, Feifei. "China Sets Subsidy for Solar Pilot Projects, Daily Says." *Bloomberg*. Bloomberg, 25 July 2013. Web. 28 Aug. 2013.

[96] Howell, Thomas R., William A. Noellert, Gregory Hume, and Alan Wm Wolff. *China's Promotion of the Renewable Electric Power Equipment Industry*. Rep. National Foreign Trade Council, 1 Mar. 2010. Web. 27 Aug. 2013.

[97] Stearns, Jonathan. "Chinese Solar-Glass Makers Face Threat of EU Tariffs." *Bloomberg*. Bloomberg, 01 Mar. 2013. Web. 28 Aug. 2013.

[98] Ibid.

[99] Shen, Feifei. "Deadly China Pollution Breathes New Life Into Solar Debt." *Bloomberg*. Bloomberg, 07 Feb. 2013. Web. 28 Aug. 2013.

[100] Howell, Thomas R., William A. Noellert, Gregory Hume, and Alan Wm Wolff. *China's Promotion of the Renewable Electric Power Equipment Industry*. Rep. National Foreign Trade Council, 1 Mar. 2010. Web. 27 Aug. 2013.

[101] Chang, Shiyan, Lili Zhao, Govinda R. Timilsina, and Xiliang Zhang. *Development of Biofuels in China: Technologies, Economics and Policies*. Rep. World Bank, Oct. 2012. Web. 29 Aug. 2013.

[102] Ibid., 6.

[103] Ibid., 9.

[104] Ibid., 10.

[105] "Food Safety in China: In The Gutter." *Economist*. The Economist Newspaper, 29 Oct. 2011. Web. 29 Aug. 2013.

[106] Chang, Shiyan, Lili Zhao, Govinda R. Timilsina, and Xiliang Zhang. *Development of Biofuels in China: Technologies, Economics and Policies*. Rep. World Bank, Oct. 2012. Web. 29 Aug. 2013.

[107] Upadhyay, Yogendra Prasad, and R. B. Sharma. "Biodiesel: An Alternative Fuel and Its Emission Effect." *IOSR Journal of Mechanical and Civil Engineering* 5.3 (2013): 1-4. *IOSRJournal*. International Organization of Scientific Research, Feb. 2013. Web. 29 Aug. 2013.

[108] Chang, Shiyan, Lili Zhao, Govinda R. Timilsina, and Xiliang Zhang. *Development of Biofuels in China: Technologies, Economics and Policies*. Rep. World Bank, Oct. 2012. Web. 29 Aug. 2013.

[109] Ibid., 14.

[110] Ibid., 2.

[111] Christiaensen, Luc, and Rasmus Heltberg. *Greening China's Rural Energy: New Insights on the Potential of Smallholder Biogas*. Rep. World Bank, June 2012. Web. 29 Aug. 2013.

[112] Ibid., 8.

[113] Ibid., 15.

[114] Ibid., 16.

[115] Ma, Jun, Audrey Shi, and Michael Tong. *Big Bang Measures to Fight Air Pollution*. Rep. Deutsche Bank, 28 Feb. 2013. Web. 21

Aug. 2013.

[116] Ibid., 26.

[117] Plumer, Brad. "How the U.S. Could Influence China's Coal Habits — with Exports." *Washington Post*. The Washington Post, 01 May 2012. Web. 29 Aug. 2013.

[118] Perry, Mark J. "The Exponential Rise in 'Saudi Texas's' Oil Output Continues – Production Has Doubled in Only 27 Months!" *AEIdeas*. American Enterprise Institute, 31 July 2013. Web. 29 Aug. 2013.

[119] Park, Gary. "Increase in North American Oil Output to Depend on Pipeline Capacity: CIBC." *Platts*. McGraw Hill Financial, 17 Aug. 2012. Web. 29 Aug. 2013.

[120] Perry, Mark J. "Amazing Texas Oil Facts from the Eagle Ford Shale and Permian Basin Areas — Teenagers Are Making $75,000." *AEIdeas*. American Enterprise Institute, 15 Mar. 2013. Web. 29 Aug. 2013.

[121] Bass, Frank. "Eagle Ford Shale Boom Fuels 'Madhouse' in South Texas Counties." *Bloomberg*. Bloomberg, 15 Mar. 2013. Web. 29 Aug. 2013.

[122] Chen, Aizhu. "China's Ragtag Shale Army a Long Way from Revolution." *Reuters*. Thomson Reuters, 10 Mar. 2013. Web. 27 Aug. 2013.

[123] Wang, Zhongying, Jingli Shi, and Yongqiang Zhao. *Technology Roadmap: China Wind Energy Development Roadmap 2050*. Rep. International Energy Agency, Oct. 2011. Web. 28 Aug. 2013.

[124] Zhang, Junfeng, Dr., Denise L. Mauzerall, Dr., Tong Zhu, Dr.,

Song Liang, Dr., Majid Ezzati, Dr., and Justin V. Remais, Dr. *Environmental Health in China: Progress towards Clean Air and Safe Water*. Rep. China Water Risk, 27 Mar. 2010. Web. 22 Aug. 2013.

[125] Perkowski, Jack. "Shale Gas: China's Untapped Resource." *Forbes*. Forbes Magazine, 13 June 2013. Web. 29 Aug. 2013.

[126] Ibid.

[127] Chen, Aizhu. "China's Ragtag Shale Army a Long Way from Revolution." *Reuters*. Thomson Reuters, 10 Mar. 2013. Web. 27 Aug. 2013.

[128] *Draft Plan to Study the Potential Impacts of Hydraulic Fracturing on Drinking Water Resources*. Rep. United States Environmental Protection Agency, Feb. 2011. Web. 29 Aug. 2013.

[129] Feodoroff, Timothe, and Jennifer Franco. "Chinese Fracking Plans Prompt "water-grabbing" Fears." *China Dialogue*. China Dialogue, 11 Mar. 2013. Web. 27 Aug. 2013.

[130] Katakey, Rakteem, Aibing Guo, and Sarah Chen. "China Joining U.S. Shale Renaissance With $40 Billion." *Bloomberg*. Bloomberg, 06 Mar. 2013. Web. 26 Aug. 2013.

[131] Ibid.

[132] Haas, Benjamin, and Rakteem Katakey. "China's Shale Gas No Revolution as Price Imperils Output: Energy." *Bloomberg*. Bloomberg, 19 Feb. 2013. Web. 27 Aug. 2013.

[133] Chen, Aizhu. "China's Ragtag Shale Army a Long Way from Revolution." *Reuters*. Thomson Reuters, 10 Mar. 2013. Web. 27

Aug. 2013.

[134] Feodoroff, Timothe, and Jennifer Franco. "Chinese Fracking Plans Prompt "water-grabbing" Fears." *China Dialogue*. China Dialogue, 11 Mar. 2013. Web. 27 Aug. 2013.

Reforms for a Better Environment

[1] OECD (2013), *OECD Economic Surveys: China 2013*, OECD Publishing. *http://dx.doi.org/10.1787/eco_surveys-chn-2013-en*

[2] Ibid., 130.

[3] Ibid., 131.

[4] Ibid.

[5] Ibid., 133.

[6] Ibid., 132.

[7] Tatlow, Didi Kirsten. "Worse Than Poisoned Water: Dwindling Water, in China's North." *New York Times*. New York Times, 5 Feb. 2013. Web. 29 Aug. 2013.

[8] OECD (2013), *OECD Economic Surveys: China 2013*, OECD Publishing. *http://dx.doi.org/10.1787/eco_surveys-chn-2013-en*

[9] Ibid., 134.

[10] Ibid., 135.

[11] Ibid., 137.

[12] Schultz, Abby. "China's CO2 Market Experiment Faces Time and Price Imperatives." *CleanBiz*. CleanBiz Asia, 30 Jan. 2013. Web. 30

Aug. 2013.

[13] Anderson, Mike, and Pratish Narayanan. "Carbon Traders Stung by Rout Try Again in China: Energy Markets." *Bloomberg.* Bloomberg, 18 Jan. 2013. Web. 30 Aug. 2013.

[14] OECD (2013), *OECD Economic Surveys: China 2013*, OECD Publishing. *http://dx.doi.org/10.1787/eco_surveys-chn-2013-en*

[15] Ibid., 147.

[16] Ministry of Finance. *Report on the Implementation of Central and Local Budgets in 2012 and on Draft of Central and Local Budgets for 2013*. Rep. N.p.: n.p., 2013.*Report on the Implementation of Central and Local Budgets in 2012 and on Draft of Central and Local Budgets for 2013*. Wall Street Journal, 5 Mar. 2013. Web. 30 Aug. 2013.

[17] Liu, Jianqiang. "China's Environment Ministry an "Utter Disappointment"" *China Dialogue*. China Dialogue, 7 Mar. 2013. Web. 30 Aug. 2013.

[18] Woetzel, Jonathan, Lenny Mendonca, Janamitra Devan, Stefano Negri, Yangmei Hu, Luke Jordan, Xiujun Li, Alexander Maasry, Geoff Tsen, and Flora Yu. *Preparing for China's Urban Billion*. Rep. McKinsey & Company, Mar. 2009. Web. 22 Aug. 2013.